Intergenerational Faith Formation

All Ages Learning Together

Mariette Martineau, Joan Weber,
& Leif Kehrwald

Intergenerational
Faith
Formation

All Ages Learning Together

TWENTY
THIRD 23rd
PUBLICATIONS

Twenty-Third Publications
A Division of Bayard
One Montauk Avenue, Suite 200
New London, CT 06320
(860) 437-3012 or (800) 321-0411
www.23rdpublications.com

The Scripture passages contained herein are from the *New Revised Standard Version of the Bible*, copyright ©1989, by the Division of Christian Education of the National Council of Churches in the U.S.A. All rights reserved.

ISBN 978-1-58595-653-1
Library of Congress Catalog Card Number: 2007939317
Printed in the U.S.A.

CONTENTS

Introduction

People, especially children and teens, learn best in developmentally appropriate settings. Wouldn't you agree? This is certainly what I learned in my education courses in college in the late 1970s. I learned the same concept in my youth ministry training courses in the 1980s. And all this was reinforced from my children's teachers in the 1990s. And, of course, it's pretty much what you'll hear from the education experts of the new millennium.

But in each of those decades, there's been a nagging contradiction to the strict developmental approach to education. Do we give children, teens, and adults enough credit for their ability to glean and learn in settings that cut across developmental lines? Do we give children enough credit for absorbing key learnings from experiences that were not specifically designed to address their developmental needs, concerns, tasks? And with respect to faith formation, how do children, adolescents, even adults *identify* with and *integrate* into the faith community when their learning is separate and segmented?

In response to the questions, we first believe that people learn the way they live. Home, church, and community (all of which are intergenerational) are the places where people learn best. When an intentional learning program reflects the nature and qualities of ordinary living, all ages can more readily enter into the educational experience.

There's no question that developmental theory, as applied in the last fifty years, has been a great asset to education, particularly for adolescents and children. But have we allowed the education pendulum to swing too far to the developmental side, to the exclusion of intergenerational learning, which, quite frankly, can at times be magical, powerful, and dramatic?

Reflect for a moment on how ancient peoples learned. Wasn't it much more relational, communal, and familial than our systematic, school house, age "appropriate" mode of education today? In fact, even today in cultures we might consider "less sophisticated" than our own, most learning takes place in the context of family and community, rather than separating children from society, dropping them into a fabricated environment—all of which is, of course, developmentally appropriate—and pumping them full of information. Do you suppose children of ancient peoples ever asked, "When will I ever need to know this?"

The purpose of this book is to show that not only is there a place for intergenerational learning in effective faith formation, there is a *necessity* for it. We contend that it is necessary not only for children, but for all ages: children, teens, young adults, adults, elderly, parents, grandparents, everyone.

Magic happens when we bring the generations together. It is not neat and tidy; rather, it is chaotic and messy. Yet our work with nearly 1500 parishes in seventy or more dioceses across North America shows us that people—children, teens, *and* adults—learn a great deal in intergenerational settings and *enjoy themselves* while doing so.

Many parish leaders are discovering that for over thirty years the Catholic Church has offered a comprehensive and compelling vision of faith formation and learning—lifelong, for all ages and generations, rooted in the life of the church. Embracing the vision of faith formation in the *General Directory for Catechesis* requires moving away from the schooling paradigm to a community or "whole church" paradigm of faith formation. Intergenerational learning is a key method to help us embrace this vision and bring it to practical reality.

We don't mean to be simplistic. Just bringing persons of various ages and stages together in the same room for faith learning is *not* the magic bullet that will solve all of today's catechetical problems. Yet, parish faith formation that engages the whole community in a journey through the core curriculum of Catholic faith, rooted in the events of church life, has the potential for responding effectively to most existing catechetical problems of our day. And the primary (though not the only) *method* for engaging the whole community in that core curriculum is intergenerational learning. It is a means to an end, not the end itself.

The *General Directory for Catechesis* reminds us, "it should not be overlooked that the recipient of catechesis is the whole Christian community and every person in it" (#168). Intergenerational learning provides an opportunity to gather the whole parish to learn, pray, celebrate, and share. What's the most important activity of the faith community? Worship, right? What's the method for gathering the community to worship? Do we put them in age-segmented, developmentally appropriate settings? No. The most important thing we do as a faith community we do together, *everybody all together!* In a similar fashion, we have discovered that learning about our faith *all together* has a profound and positive impact on the life of the community.

With this vision of lifelong faith formation for the whole community and with this method of intergenerational learning, we seek to...

- transform the focus on children-only (think of all the time, energy, and resources we commit to children only) by implementing lifelong faith formation for all ages and generations, including and especially adults

- transform "start and stop" catechesis (think graduation at confirmation; think preparation for sacraments) by implementing lifelong and continuous faith formation—learning for a lifetime through involvement in the events of church life

- transform age segregation (think grade levels or groups: youth group, older adults group) by implementing intergenerational faith formation—making connections among the generations in learning programs and parish involvement

- transform the focus on the "textbook as the curriculum" by utilizing the events of church life as the curriculum for all ages and generations—tapping into the educative and transformative power of the church year, sacramental celebrations, community prayer, and works of justice and service *and* providing catechesis that prepares everyone to learn by participating in the events of church life

- transform the attitude of blaming families for our current situation—
the "family's faith is the problem"—by nurturing family faith at home
as integral to faith formation
- transform catechesis as a separate "program" by implementing a
more collaborative and integrated approach that involves all of the
parish's ministries in faith formation.

Effective catechesis is interconnected with liturgy, sacraments, the church year, justice and service, prayer—and utilizes intergenerational learning as a key method for implementation.

What We Are Learning

In the spring of 2005, we conducted a comprehensive research survey of parishes engaged in the *Generations of Faith* approach to lifelong faith formation. Using both quantitative and qualitative research methods, we gathered data from nearly 1000 parishes from all across North America. All of these parishes were utilizing intergenerational learning as a key method of implementation.

Our research yielded a plethora of findings and conclusions on all aspects of this innovative faith-formation effort. Here, we want to share with you the findings related to intergenerational learning.

- Parishes are having success in engaging all ages in faith formation,
especially parents and other adults. They now have a lifelong
curriculum that provides foundational catechesis for everyone.
- Parishioners of all ages are developing a deeper understanding of
the foundational themes of the Catholic faith—church year, liturgy
and sacraments, creed, morality, prayer, justice—and learning how
to live their faith in the parish, at home, and in the world.
- Parishes are having success with the intergenerational learning
model, gathering parishioners of all the generations to learn
together. Many parishes are pleasantly surprised by the high level of
participation and the positive response from parishioners of all ages.
And they are attracting large numbers of adults: middle-aged adults
without children and older adults!

- Parishioners are beginning to build relationships with people across all of the ages, and this is benefiting the entire parish community.
- Parents are participating with their children, often for the first time, and are finding benefit in learning together as a family. Families are beginning to incorporate faith sharing activities at home.

Leaders from these parishes recognize the value of building a supportive faith community among all the generations. They recognize that intergenerational learning provides an opportunity to gather the whole parish to learn, pray, celebrate, and share. And they see benefits to the community as wells as to individuals. Specifically, these benefits include:

- building community and meaningful relationships across all the generations in a parish
- providing a setting for each generation to share and learn from the other generations (their faith, stories, wisdom, experience, and knowledge); the parent and grandparent generations pass on the traditions of family and faith to the younger generations; while the younger generations share their faith, energy, and new insights with the parent and grandparent generations
- providing an environment where new ways of living one's faith can be practiced
- providing adult role models for children and youth
- promoting understanding of shared values and a common faith, as well as respect for individuals in all stages and ages of life
- helping to overcome the age-segregated nature of our society and church programs.

These features of intergenerational faith formation are explored in greater detail in Chapter One.

In This Book

This book has been a group effort on the part of those of us who work with the *Generations of Faith* project. All of us have learned a great deal about intergenerational faith formation in the last five years.

We are convinced that it is a necessary, crucial, and effective tool for catechesis. Each contributing author brings a different lens of expertise to understand the nuances and complexities of intergenerational learning and the implications for effective lifelong learning for the whole community.

This book serves as a companion to three other books that we at the Center for Ministry Development have written. These document the development of the *Generations of Faith* project (GOF).

- *Generations of Faith Resource Manual: Lifelong Faith Formation for the Whole Parish Community* by John Roberto and Mariette Martineau

- *Generations of Faith Sourcebook: Lifelong Faith Formation for the Whole Parish Community* by John Roberto

- *Families and Faith: A Vision and Practice for Parish Leaders* edited by Leif Kehrwald

These three books—also published by Twenty-Third Publications—articulate the vision and break open the mechanics of implementing event-centered, lifelong, intergenerational faith formation in the parish. This book, *Intergenerational Faith Formation*, explores the key method for fulfilling this overarching vision.

In this book, you will read about the following:

- Chapter One addresses the context and urgency for intergenerational faith formation. This chapter looks at the critical need for intergenerational learning in today's church, and offers what some parishes have to say about their experience in utilizing this method.

- Chapters Two and Three take a look at how people learn today, current theories for learning, and principles for effective learning that are age, gender, and culture inclusive. These chapters make a case for intergenerational learning as one of the ways in which people learn best.

- Chapter Four outlines the theory that supports intergenerational learning. It explores the necessary elements that need to be present for persons of all ages to learn in a multigenerational context. This chapter also highlights some common pitfalls and mistakes. And

Chapter Five explores theological foundations for intergenerational faith formation.

- Chapters Six and Seven explore the current practice of inter-generational faith formation in the church today. These chapters offer examples and stories from parishes implementing intergenerational faith formation and explore their catechetical effectiveness. Based on data from our qualitative and quantitative research of *Generations of Faith* parishes, the reader will see what is entailed in the transition from a schooling model to an intergenerational model of faith formation.

- Chapter Eight breaks open the nuts and bolts of implementing intergenerational faith formation in the parish. These chapters explore ways to incorporate intergenerational learning into the parish's systematic catechetical plan, specifically with respect to such programs as sacramental preparation, vacation Bible school, parish mission, and so on. In an effort to articulate the critical practices necessary for fruitful implementation of intergenerational faith learning, these chapters will include real-life parish stories.

As with all of our publications, this book is intended to be a discussion starter rather than the final word. Read it. Discuss it with your colleagues. Engage in the practice of intergenerational learning, and let us know what you learn. You are on the front lines of catechetical ministry. You know how to make things work in your particular community. Share your feedback with us, and we will pass it along to others who are also anxious to succeed. Send your comments directly to me, Leif Kehrwald, at *lkehrwald@cmdnet.org*.

About the Center for Ministry Development

Founded in 1978, the Center for Ministry Development is an independent, non-profit organization whose core purpose is to bring the Good News in new ways to the people of God. CMD's mission is to empower faith communities and their leaders for effective ministry with youth, young adults, and families through ministry education, ministry development training, programs, and publications.

CHAPTER ONE

Context and Urgency for Intergenerational Faith Formation

Imagine that it is Tuesday evening of the third week of Lent. Imagine that the largest gathering space at your parish is filled with people of all ages: persons in their eighties who have been members of the parish for fifty years or more, unattached adults, empty nesters, and parents with their school-age children, young couples and singles in their twenties and thirties. Even the teens are there in full force.

Imagine that at the front of the room, there is a beautifully designed prayer space with symbols of the Triduum prominently displayed.

There is energy in the room and people are happy to be together. They are seated at round tables, with all of the different generations represented at each table. A catechist with a genuine gift for teaching gives a powerful explanation of the meaning of Jesus' washing his apostles' feet at the Last Supper. The catechist then invites the table groups to apply the teaching to their lives as disciples. Later, people seem truly uplifted when a seven-year-old gets up in front of the whole assembly and shares what "washing feet" means to him.

One cannot fully describe the power of a well-designed and executed faith formation session that involves the whole parish community.

It's not just the joy and the energy and the interaction, although all of these elements are present. It is the sense that people are claiming their baptismal call, learning their faith but also sharing it with others. One pastor said it well, describing how he feels when he enters the room where intergenerational faith formation is taking place, "It's a joy to be in the midst of joy!"

Sense of Urgency

The twenty-first century has witnessed a movement in the church toward catechesis that encompasses much more than the traditional child-centered classroom model. Many parishes are embracing faith formation that involves all ages learning together as they witness to their faith. Driving this transition is a sense of urgency that we need to do something different because our current catechetical methods are not working. Studies of the fifty percent of the church population who are postmoderns—those born after 1960 and raised in the post-Vatican II era—reveal that they are not as involved in church life and worship as previous generations. They are "cafeteria Catholics" who feel perfectly comfortable picking and choosing which church beliefs they will embrace and which they will leave behind. And they struggle to find the relevance of the Catholic faith to their everyday lives.

Today's young parents are all postmoderns; they grew up in a world in which Christianity was just one voice, and often not the most dominant one, among a variety of voices bombarding them with choices. Many of them yearn to pass the faith on to their children, but lack the vocabulary, the support, and the resources to do so. Intergenerational faith formation experiences in the parish, in which parents are catechized with their children, can give them the confidence and skills they need to do faith-sharing at home. As one leader in a parish which moved from classroom-only to intergenerational faith formation described it:

> I think another big change has been that we've empowered parents to pass on the faith to their children. We've done this by teaching them about their faith and they're learning and therefore when they get into the car and they drive home they can share the topic with their kids. They know what they're talking about and they feel empowered because they're able to

do what they promised at baptism and pass their faith on to their children. (CMD)

Searching for ways to make catechesis more effective in forming Christian disciples, catechetical leaders are turning to the vision for faith formation articulated in contemporary church documents. The *General Directory for Catechesis* and the *National Directory for Catechesis* both identify the importance of the community's role in lifelong catechesis as both teacher and learner. Parishes are finding ways to put that theory into practice through intergenerational experiences. They are taking seriously the church's teaching that faith formation is lifelong and that the aim of catechesis is "intimacy and communion with Jesus Christ" (GDC, #80).

Also, faith formation leaders are examining our rich tradition and history and recognizing that we are failing in the art of passing on the faith, which previous generations practiced so seamlessly. They are looking for ways to live out the wonderful description of faith formation in Psalm 78:

> Attend, my people, to my teaching: listen to the words of my mouth. I will open my mouth in story, drawing lessons from of old. We have heard them, we know them; our ancestors have recited them to us. We do not keep them from our children; we recite them to the next generation, the praiseworthy and mighty deeds of the Lord, the wonders that he performed. God set up a decree in Jacob, established a law in Israel: What he commanded our ancestors, they were to teach their children; that the next generation might come to know, children yet to be born. In turn they were to recite them to their children, that they too might put their trust in God, and not forget the works of God, keeping his commandments. (Psalm 78:1–7)

This chapter seeks to identify and explore the practical and ecclesial reasons for an intergenerational approach to faith formation and the benefits of such an approach.

The Value of Intergenerational Experiences

We live today in a society where it is hard for people of different generations to interact—even within their own families. Many young families live far from their parents and grandparents, diminishing the opportunities for storytelling, sharing memories, and passing on faith and family traditions. Learning and recreation tend to happen along age lines. Even worship can sometimes be generation-specific. (Consider the average age at the early Sunday morning Mass, or by contrast, think about who comes to the late Sunday afternoon liturgy.)

The Search Institute, in partnership with the Lutheran Brotherhood, did a national study on how well American adults relate to young people. When asked which actions they felt were important in connecting with children, the adults surveyed identified such things as teaching shared values, guiding decision making, holding meaningful conversations, and discussing personal values. One of the conclusions of the study was this:

> Despite a broad consensus among American adults about what they should do for kids, few adults actually do these things. The alarming gap between what adults believe kids need and what adults actually do shows that we're not providing kids with the relationships and support necessary to grow up healthy. (Scales, Benson, and Roehlkepartain)

It certainly lies within the purview of the church to provide opportunities for adults and children to connect on things like values and discernment. Intergenerational faith formation is ideally situated to respond to the gap the Search Institute study revealed.

Another reality in the world that argues for more intergenerational interaction is the growing population of senior citizens in our country. Temple University's Center for Intergenerational Learning has researched the elders in our communities, including the rich contributions which senior citizens *could be* making in their communities. The Center describes the value of intergenerational experiences on its website:

> Many older people are seeking opportunities to share their skills, knowledge, and experiences with younger generations. They are an invaluable source of support for young people who need caring adults to guide and nurture them as they navigate the difficult course to adulthood....Intergenerational programs and policies are valuable approaches for addressing critical social problems, ensuring the transmission of culture across

generations, and building stronger communities. (Temple University Center for Intergenerational Learning)

It is important to note that the Center for Intergenerational Learning supports *mutual* learning and growth in intergenerational experiences. It is not just the elders providing wisdom to naïve young people. It is different generations together striving to be "community" in the best possible way. Parishes, called to be genuine communities of support and interaction, could utilize intergenerational faith formation to set the stage for this type of sharing.

One catechetical leader who is a practitioner of intergenerational faith formation describes how the generations learn from each other this way:

> It has really helped me to appreciate the wisdom of our seniors, the energy and faithfulness and spirit of our children, the hunger of our parents, and the questioning of our young adults. We bring all that together in a community setting and allow them to minister to each other and to help each other grow, and then take it home with them. (CMD)

Another value in intergenerational learning sessions is the opportunity for the community to learn from each other's experiences of God. Hearing a woman with breast cancer describe the power of prayer provides a profound awareness of God's loving care in our lives. Listening to a teen describe what solidarity with the poor and vulnerable means to him, after experiencing the faith of the poor in a soup kitchen, can be transformative for all age groups. And watching the eighty-year-old who attends daily liturgy share what Eucharist means in her life can lead to a more meaningful experience of liturgy for those who hear her story.

When the *National Directory for Catechesis* describes effective methodologies for catechesis today, it includes human experience as "a constituent element in catechesis" (USCCB #29, 97). The NDC advocates (for cross-generational sharing of faith) using as an example the value of tapping into the faithful witness of the elderly: "In light of the courageous and faithful witness they have born to the Gospel over many years, the elderly are natural catechists, especially for their own grandchildren. Their unique catechesis has the invaluable element of intergenerational dialogue that adds a significant dimension to the proclamation of the

Gospel within the family and within the community of faith" (NDC #48B, p. 195). It is exciting to witness the convergence of thinking between the church teachings on intergenerational sharing and the research of groups like Temple University's Center for Intergenerational Learning.

Compelling Research

Much of the motivation for seeking a new way of doing catechesis is generated by the sobering statistics on participation in church life of the first postmodern generations in history. These children, youth, and young adults are the members of our parishes who were born after 1960 and include two distinct cohort groups: Generation Xers and the Millennials who follow them. Together they comprise about half of the Catholic population. The research of Dean Hoge, James Davidson, William D'Antonio, and Mary Gautier on these generations and how they compare to older generations of Catholics is addressed in their book *American Catholics Today: New Realities of Their Faith and Their Church*. Their research indicates that weekly Mass attendance decreases dramatically across generations, with 60% of pre-Vatican II Catholics (born before 1940), 35% of Vatican II Catholics (born between 1940 and 1960), 26% of Generation Xers (born between 1961 and 1978), and only 15% of Millennials attending regularly.

We can no longer count on Sunday Mass as a contact point with the majority of Catholics. We still believe that Sunday worship is the source and summit of our lives as disciples of Christ; but if the majority of people do not attend, how can we expect them to engage in their faith communities—for catechesis or any other element of church life?

In addition to the decline in Sunday Mass attendance, the researchers noted a decline in other faith practices and a change in the acceptance of doctrine and creedal beliefs that traditionally defined the boundaries of our faith. Many Catholics feel comfortable disagreeing with church teachings on such issues as abortion, birth control, and divorce.

While there are many examples of exemplary catechetical programs for children and adolescents in our church, it is clear that more is needed to counter the effects of secularism, consumerism, and all the other realities that draw people away from their faith. Since people live with these challenges in their daily lives, it makes sense to have them learn their faith response in intergenerational settings as well. Doing faith formation with all ages together reinforces the connection to other aspects of our lives because it is the way we worship, the way we work, and the way we interact in our families.

There has never been a stronger need for intergenerational faith formation. Today's culture makes it hard for people to learn from other age groups. The pure, unfiltered faith of the very young is not heard by youth, young adults, and older adults because children are taught in age-segregated ways. The challenges and questions of youth and young adults are not heard by older generations because, outside of youth ministry, Catholic schools, and programs like "Theology on Tap," the questions are not being asked in broader church settings. When we bring the different age groups together, we see a revitalization of the faith of the elders and a deeper understanding of the faith traditions on the part of the young.

William D. Dinges, in his chapter on "Faith, Hope, and (Excessive) Individualism" in *Handing on the Faith: The Church's Mission and Challenge*, describes another contemporary challenge the church faces in transmitting the faith. He writes about the lack of a Catholic culture in which young people can be apprenticed into the faith. This is dramatically different from how many, if not most, older Catholics experienced their faith. For pre-Vatican II and Vatican II Catholics, there was a unique and defined Catholic culture. The church was an integral part of their everyday lives. People grew up in Catholic neighborhoods, went to Catholic schools, and were taught Catholic values at home and in the parish. But today, "Minus the experience of Catholicism as a vibrant social reality (symbolically understood in the imagery of the "Body of Christ"), young Catholics are less likely to be successfully socialized into the tradition, less likely to find it compelling, less likely to have a bounded sense of identity, less likely to develop a Catholic vocabulary to interpret their experiences, and less likely to find the tradition's plausibility structures credible" (Imbelli, p. 42).

Dinges points out that the solution is more than a cognitive task, more than giving young people information about their Catholic religion. He says that the solution is, instead, sociological. "It means addressing the atrophy of communal participation and the need for a socially embedded Catholicism. It includes the creative (re)construction and intensification of Catholicism as a *communal* reality of habit, prayer, reflection, dialogue, and debate. It necessitates the (re)creation of more cohesive social bonds, shared memories, mutual responsibilities, permanent relationships, and other experiences of connectedness" (p. 43).

Dinges' insights can lead to a thoughtful consideration of where and how to create intergenerational experiences for our parishioners. Bringing all ages together to learn and share their faith can only contribute to the reconstruction of the Catholic culture which Dinges describes. When done well, intergenerational learning includes the elements of practice, prayer, reflection, dialogue, and sometimes even debate.

The Parish as Community

Sister Edith Prendergast, RSC, Director of the Office of Religious Education in the Archdiocese of Los Angeles, believes that the right foundation for doing faith formation with the whole community needs to be laid first. That foundation as described in *A Pastor's Guide to Whole Community Catechesis*, is "an ecclesiology of communion. We are called to a *communion* of ordered relationships….This brings us to understanding the parish as a web of interlocking relationships all focused on the community as a learning, questioning, celebrating, welcoming, and evangelizing community of faith" (Huebsch, p. 41).

And that is what happens when parishes make intergenerational catechesis integral in their faith formation efforts. As one Generations of Faith parish leader put it:

> Since we started GOF, I see more people talking to one another after Mass and spending time together. We recognize people as a staff; they recognize us. It's just building relationships and community within a parish. (CMD)

Clearly, a compelling reason for doing intergenerational faith formation is the way it helps build community within the parish. We Catholics are a communal group. We believe in a Triune God who lives in and as community. The Second Person of the Trinity, incarnated as Jesus, fulfilled his earthly mission in and through a community of twelve apostles. The early church, on fire with the Spirit, lived in almost perfect community, learning and growing in faith together:

> They devoted themselves to the teaching of the apostles and to the communal life, to the breaking of the bread and to the prayers. Awe came upon everyone, and many wonders and signs were done through the apostles. All who believed were together and had all things in common; they would sell their property and possessions and divide them among all according to each one's need. Every day they devoted themselves to meeting together in the temple area and to breaking bread in their homes. They ate their meals with exultation and sincerity of heart, praising God and enjoying favor with all the people. And every day the Lord added to their number those who were being saved. (Acts 2:42–47)

Bringing people together to learn the core curriculum of their faith creates a communal identity in parishioners. It can transform a parish into a genuine community approaching the likes of the one described in the Acts of the Apostles. As one parish leader put it:

> We are beginning to experience a real transformation in our parish community. We are starting to see more involvement with liturgical ministries from all ages, more understanding of the Mass and church year, and a much stronger sense of community. We are also more committed than ever to using GOF to "Break Open the Word" from Sunday liturgy. It is a huge key to keeping our formation and liturgical life unified. (CMD)

In her insightful book *Fashion Me a People,* Maria Harris wrote that the curriculum of the church is really the "*entire course of the church's life,* found in the fundamental forms of that life. It is the priestly, prophetic, and political work of *didache, leiturgia, koinonia, kerygma,* and *diakonia*" (Harris, p. 64). She makes a strong case for all five forms, but sees *koinonia,* or community, as the starting point in educational ministry. With that in mind, doesn't it make sense to fashion the core curriculum of the parish—the most important beliefs and practices of our faith—in such a way that the intergenerational community learns it together and teaches it to each other as members grow in love for their God, their faith, and their community?

Charles Foster, in *Educating Congregations,* uses the wisdom of Walter Brueggemann to assert that one purpose of church education is binding the different generations within the congregation into community. "In the congregation's elders, those who are young in age and faith discover clues to the identity and mission of the church. Through the youth of the congregation, the elders envision the community's continuity and renewal. If church education is not intensely intergenerational, the 'continuity' of its 'vision, value, and perception' cannot be maintained over time or renewed for changing circumstances" (Foster, p. 62). Making our catechetical efforts "intensely intergenerational" holds the potential for meeting the faith and community hungers of people in the twenty-first century.

A faith formation leader in North Dakota shared her conviction that intergenerational faith formation only works if the community believes that God speaks through all age groups, including children. One of the gifts of cross-generational learning is that each age group gets the opportunity to share its unique perspective on faith with other generations and to learn from the lived experience of those older and younger. The question each faith community must ask itself before venturing into intergenerational faith formation is this: Do we believe that God speaks through each member of our faith community, from the innocent child to the restless teenager, from the questioning young adult to the faithful elder? If so, awesome things can happen and parishioners may discover that their Gabriel (God's messenger) is the person sitting at the table with them at their next intergenerational faith formation session.

The Church's Vision

The documents of the church following the Second Vatican Council make a strong case for communal learning of the faith. The *General Directory for Catechesis* called for a lifelong approach to catechesis, which places adult faith formation at the core of our catechetical efforts and makes the community the source, means, and locus for our catechetical efforts. The *National Directory for Catechesis,* building on the GDC, identified the church as both the "principal agent of catechesis and the primary recipient of catechesis" (#47, 186). The bishops write that "The witness of the Christian community—particularly the parish, family, parents, and catechists—is an important element in catechetical methodology. The effectiveness of catechesis depends to a great extent on the vitality of the

Christian community in which it is given" (NDC #29C, p. 100). If the research shows that we lack a Catholic culture in which to apprentice our younger generations into the faith, then we need to live the spirit of the church documents by creating intergenerational opportunities in the parish for learning the faith.

While age-specific learning will always be needed because of the developmental differences in each age group, the classroom model alone is not capable of creating a community of learners which the church documents envision. Charles Foster described the flaws in the current Christian educational system:

- Loss of a "corporate memory" of our faith tradition;
- Failure to teach the relevance of the Bible to everyday life;
- Reducing religious education to a *program* rather than a way of life into which people are mentored and apprenticed;
- Being held captive by the dominant culture in which the Good News is being shared;
- Failure to adapt our educational strategies to the changing world in which we live (Foster, pp. 22-35).

Intergenerational learning is uniquely situated to provide solutions to Foster's first and third flaws. When people of different ages are brought together to learn their faith, the corporate memory of the faith tradition is strengthened and sustained. We can teach children how to pray the Rosary, but having them hear the stories of elders whose prayer lives were sustained by a particular Mystery, or by the rosary's pattern of praying, keeps alive the tradition and enriches the faith of all who hear the stories.

Seeing religious education as a way of life into which people are mentored requires a mentoring relationship. It challenges us to put young people in touch with "wisdom people" in the community who have mastered a particular aspect of discipleship—be it having a preferential option for the poor, praying well, making ethical decisions in the workplace or the shopping mall, or evangelizing others.

Noted theologian and catechetical leader Thomas Groome also affirms the positive values of bringing the whole community together to learn and share their faith. He wrote that "our contemporary situation poses tremendous challenges to 'handing on the faith'. . . Though we can never return to the 'good old days,' we must retain the insight reflected there—it still takes a family and a village to raise a Christian. We simply need to be more intentional and find contemporary ways to do whole community catechesis" (Imbelli, 178). If intergenerational faith formation experiences help parents raise faithful children, that in itself makes the effort worthwhile.

Groome also built on Karl Rahner's insight that Vatican II redefined our view of faith. Rahner recognized that if faith is narrowly defined as belief in doctrines, catechesis could be done by a teacher with a catechism instructing a classroom of children. But the Second Vatican Council reclaimed the early church's understanding of Christian faith, reminding us that genuine faith engages the whole person—one's identity—and is at the same time "radically communal" (p. 178).

Groome's analysis of catechesis is rooted in scripture:

> The communal nature of being Christian was evident from the beginning, with roots in God's call to Abraham and Sarah to become the parents of a people. The first Christians had such a communal understanding of their identity that Paul used the rich metaphor of the human body to describe them, urging all members to work together as the Body of Christ, alive by the Spirit in the world. . . Vatican II was a watershed in returning Catholics to the communal nature of Christian faith, and to the agency of each baptized member for the mission of the church in the world. Over and over it restated in one way or another that the church must function as a community, and that all the baptized 'share in the priestly, prophetic, and royal office of Christ'. . . These dual emphases of Christian faith—holistic and communal—make imperative the proactive participation of family and parish in catechetical education. (p. 179)

Groome's conclusion is that total catechetical education demands the following:

- "an intentional coalition of 'family,' 'parish,' and 'program/school'
- involving all aspects of each—their whole communal life
- engaging all members as teachers and learners, sharing faith together

- across the life-cycle from cradle to grave—in 'permanent catechesis' (GDC)
- informing and forming each other's identity in whole and communal Christian faith
- as disciples of Jesus Christ for God's reign in the world" (p. 181).

This is a thorough and compelling explanation of the elements involved in all ages learning their faith together.

Groome will always be known for his advocacy of approaching faith formation within the context of the learner's life experience. Groome wrote, "Over many years, my own work has attempted to articulate a 'shared Christian praxis approach' to catechesis and religious education" (p. 189). That is not new thinking on his part. But his contemporary reflection on the state of religious education in the church today leads him to a new conclusion about how to do praxis: "The ideal context of this approach is a community of conversation and active participation by all in sharing and learning faith together" (189).

Imagine what your faith community would be like if it lived up to this description, if it could genuinely be called a "community of conversation and active participation by all in sharing and learning faith together."

Creating a Thirst for God

Bishop Blaise Cupich, Bishop of Rapid City, has written about the decision in his diocese to move toward intergenerational faith formation. His reflections, "Handing on the Faith through Community-Based Faith Formation," are included in *Handing on the Faith: The Church's Mission and Challenge.* Bishop Cupich acknowledged that the old method of catechesis isn't enough for today. He described the anxiety of many Catholics about passing on the faith to the next generations and their recognition that what we have been doing is not working. He believes that a fresh approach must address three issues: "We need to pass on the faith in a way that creates a thirst for God and the church in the lives of young people....Consideration has to be given to the context of church life and practice when it comes to sharing the content of our faith and tradition....The participation and witness of everyone is needed. Everyone is responsible and has to be involved. We found such a design in the intergenerational/ecclesial models" that many dioceses are beginning to use (Imbelli, p. 198).

Bishop Cupich addressed the consequences and implications of shifting from a schooling model of catechesis to a community-based faith formation model. He included these points:

- Everyone is responsible with an intergenerational approach because "all take responsibility for creating the circumstances for handing on the faith to all. That means that faith formation is not just for the young. It is intergenerational because faith formation is a matter of lifelong learning."

- The context for learning the content of faith is the events in the life of the church.

- The events-centered, lifelong approach involves a systematic and cyclical curriculum over a six-year period.

- What happens at home reinforces what takes place in the community as it learns and develops a corporate Catholic identity (pp. 199-200).

The Family Connection

One of the most compelling reasons for doing intergenerational faith formation lies in Bishop Cupich's last point, that the domestic church can reinforce the faith learned in the parish. Life in the twenty-first century is hectic, and families are torn in many directions—including their own work and social lives and the school activities, sports, and social activities of their children. When the church carves out time for families to learn together in the parish, then sends them home with resources to continue their journey at home, there is a greater chance for faith-sharing to happen. In some cases, families have had wonderful experiences of shared faith in their sacramental preparation programs. But more is needed.

An additional challenge to busy families is the awareness by parents that they just don't know how to have that faith conversation with their children. They don't have the resources to create a home ritual. They realize that they can't give what they themselves don't have. And this reality is growing as more postmoderns begin to raise families.

In the midst of the chaos of today's families and their lives, the *Catechism of the Catholic Church* describes the role of parents in the faith formation of their children: "Parents have the first responsibility for the education of their children" (#2223). The parish owes its families two elements in the process of conversion: catechetical experiences in the parish which help families learn their Catholic identity as families; and resources to help families continue the learning of their faith at home. In the NDC, the bishops write that "Catechesis that involves the whole family is a particularly effective method of catechesis for young children because it helps parents become more confident in sharing their faith with their children and encouraging their children's emerging faith" (#48E, p. 204).

Bill Huebsch takes the family perspective further in an online article he wrote for the National Association of Catholic Family Life Ministers. Huebsch describes the challenge this way:

> We know that, without the parental role, little we do with children to form them in faith will have a lasting effect. And unless catechesis is situated within the liturgical life of the church, learners may know about religion in a cognitive sense, but lack the affective knowledge that comes only from ritual. Furthermore, we know that catechesis is a lifelong matter. It doesn't stop after First Communion or Confirmation. And we know that it must lead in the end to a lifestyle of faith, to households of faith.

Intergenerational faith formation can support families. As one practitioner put it:

> Lives have changed in the families who have participated. Their relationships with one another, their relationship with God, their relationship with the church—total transformation. (CMD)

This total transformation can happen because families are on the same page regarding the content of their faith. They have learned together in the intergenerational sessions, and are sent home with resources to continue that learning and apply it to their own lives as family.

Conclusion

No one would argue that we need to do more to bring our faith communities together, to learn our faith on a deeper level, to practice that faith with enthusiasm and fidelity, to support families in sharing faith at home, and to respond in conversion as disciples of Christ. It is hard work, or course, to shape the core curriculum of the parish around intergenerational learning and then mesh the age-specific learning needs of each cohort group with the core. But it is worth it. Blessed moments occur when faith sharing happens across the generations. One practitioner summed it up very vividly:

> Families feel empowered to bring faith and traditions into the home, and adults expect a high level of catechetical content especially in bulletins and home resources. The sense of care and community has helped to bring about more vibrant liturgies. Sunday attendance has grown by 20% in a year. (CMD)

Intergenerational learning, done well, brings all ages together to learn and share faith. It leads to a greater sense of community among parishioners and brings them back to the source at Sunday liturgy. The goal of catechesis, intimacy and communion with Jesus, is realized in a living and faithful way.

End Notes

Center for Ministry Development (CMD). Generations of Faith Lilly Endowment-Funded Project Evaluation, 2005. The quotes in this chapter are part of the qualitative research the Center for Ministry Development conducted as part of its final report to the Lilly Foundation. The quotes come from taped interviews with faith formation leaders and pastors in parishes which were part of the Generations of Faith Project.

Congregation for the Clergy. *General Directory for Catechesis*. Washington, DC: United States Conference of Catholic Bishops, 1998.

D'Antonio, William V, et al. *American Catholics Today: New Realities of Their Faith and Their Church*. Plymouth, UK: Roman and Littlefield, 2007.

Foster, Charles. *Educating Congregations*. Nashville, TN: Abingdon Press, 1994.

Harris, Maria. *Fashion Me a People*. Louisville: Westminster John Knox Press, 1989.

Huebsch, Bill. *A Pastor's Guide to Whole Community Catechesis.* Mystic, CT: Twenty-Third Publications, 2005.

Huebsch, Bill. "Whole Community Catechesis: Stick to the Principles," *Family Perspective Journal.* Dayton, OH: National Association of Catholic Family Life Ministers, Spring, 2006 as accessed at this Web site: http://www.nacflm.org/displaycommon.cfm?an=1&subarticlenb r=52.

Imbelli, Robert P., editor. *Handing on the Faith: The Church's Mission and Challenge.* New York: Herder & Herder, 2006.

Libreria Editrice Vaticana. *Catechism of the Catholic Church, Second Edition.* Washington, DC: United States Catholic Conference, 1997.

Scales, Peter C., Ph.D., Peter L. Benson, Ph.D., and Eugene C. Roehlkepartain. "Grading Grown Ups: American Adults Report on Their *Real* Relationships with Kids." Highlights from a Nationwide Study by Lutheran Brotherhood and Search Institute, 2001 as accessed at this web address: http://www.search-institute.org/norms/2000/ summary.pdf.

Temple University Center for Intergenerational Learning. "Why Link Generations?" Philadelphia, Pennsylvania: Temple University CIL, accessed at this web address on August 1, 2007: http://www.templecil. org/why_link_generations.

United States Conference of Catholic Bishops. *National Directory for Catechesis.* Washington, DC: USCCB Publishing, 2005.

CHAPTER TWO

Event-Centered, Intergenerational Learning

Vivendi, Credendi, and Orandi

A young couple was attending the Easter Vigil for the first time. One of their friend's wives had journeyed through the parish RCIA process throughout the year, so they came to the Vigil to support her. As they were leaving the celebration, the pastor asked them how they had enjoyed their evening. They smiled politely and said that it had been a beautiful celebration, but then humbly added that they "felt out of their league" as they did not understand all the things that had taken place.

A grandfather was taking his visiting granddaughter to Mass with him one Sunday morning. The nine-year-old had only been to church a few times, and she was constantly asking her grandfather to explain things as the Mass went on. The grandfather made several attempts to do so and then realized that he, too, was starting to wonder what things meant. A practicing Catholic all his life, he had never really taken too much time to learn about his faith.

As the parish prepared for the arrival of their refugee family, the parish refugee sponsorship committee chairperson found himself explaining again and again why the sponsorship was important and how Catholic social teachings strongly supported the parish's choice to support this family. He began to realize how little the parish knew about the social teachings of the church.

In his book *The Future of Christian Education: Educating Congregations*, Charles Foster says:

> The gospel originated in acts of God experienced as events by communities of people....Our relationship to (these) events has an educative character. If they are to become important to us, we must be familiar with them. If we are to participate in them, we must learn how to do so. If we are to be agents of their meanings, we must develop sensibilities for the roles and responsibilities needed to fulfill that task. As we try to understand these events we begin to link ideas and actions, to discover new possibilities for learning. As these events become increasingly important to us, we find ourselves developing skills to interpret other experiences through their categories and concepts. (pp. 38-39)

As alluded to in Chapter One, there is an urgency with respect to faith formation today because we are failing to form people in the faith in a manner that empowers them to practice their faith and fully participate in the events of the faith community. On the other hand, imagine the synergy of faith expression if all in the whole community were *formed* in and prepared for the same event or practice at the same time!

Charles Foster offers a framework on which to build intergenerational learning: preparing learners to participate in the events of church life (all the things we do to live out our faith—pray, worship, serve, live morally, build community, and so on), challenging learners to reflect on their experience of the actual event, and supporting learners to transform their lives as a result of the event. Since the majority of church events are intergenerational, why shouldn't the community *form* itself around those events in an intergenerational way?

Foster's insights challenge us to:

- **help church members be familiar with the events of church life** As the opening stories indicate, members need to have a familiarity with key events like the Easter Triduum and weekly Eucharist, as well as acts of justice and service.

- **share with members their roles and responsibilities as participants in the events** What does it mean to be fully, consciously, and actively celebrating Eucharist as a member of the assembly? What does one need to be able to do, know, and value to participate actively in the celebration of the Easter Vigil or to support the parish's refugee family project?

- **trust in the power of "events" to transform lives** When participants are well prepared to participate fully in the event, it can change the way they live. As just one example, one's experience of the Easter Vigil can leave an indelible mark that is carried into the world, permeating one's daily realities.

Though it is possible to create a curriculum of intergenerational learning from a variety of other frameworks: doctrinal themes, topics from children's textbooks, formation moments from household life (milestones), and so on, one of the seemingly unique elements of our approach to intergenerational faith formation is through the window of the events and practices of a community's life. Yet this is not a *new* approach but rather has been at the core of faith formation from the beginning.

As It Was in the Beginning

Lex orandi, lex credendi is an axiom coined in the fifth century, which means that the law of praying establishes the law of belief. At that time it expressed the idea that theologians were drawing on the early church's liturgical practices as a primary source for understanding Christian belief. In order to name and identify Christian beliefs, theologians turned to liturgical texts, prayers, rites, and rubrics to see the beliefs incarnated through liturgy. Pope Paul VI used the axiom following Vatican Council II to revise and re-align liturgical rites. The liturgical rites (*orandi*) were to be revised so that they would more clearly express Catholic belief and doctrine (*credendi*).

Lex orandi, lex credendi is a fundamental principle that continues to guide liturgical theology. *Orandi* refers to liturgy, the church's official public prayer, while "*credendi*" refers to the beliefs held by the church. All the central beliefs are to be expressed through the community's liturgy.

This ancient axiom has a contemporary addition, *lex vivendi*, which refers to the non-liturgical practices of Christian life. This category of practices is extensive and includes such things as service to others, work for justice and peace, personal or household prayer, study and reflection, and activities that promote the building up of the Christian community. These practices have an intrinsic connection to both the church's beliefs and its liturgy.

To put it rather simply, as individuals and as a community, we must pray what we believe; believe what we pray. Pray what we live; live what we pray. Live what we believe; believe what we live.

Even the church's catechisms have schematically lined up to *vivendi*, *orandi*, and *credendi*. Thomas Groome wrote about the axiom and the great catechisms of the church in this way:

> Christians are to love God, self, and others—the primary law of discipleship—with their whole mind, heart, and strength, and with all their soul. Throughout Christian history this wholeness of faith was reflected in the church's insistence that being Christian entails right belief (*orthodoxa*), right ethic (*orthopraxis*), and right worship (*ortholeiturgia*). Cyril of Jerusalem (d. 386) was likely the first to portray the totality of Christian faith as right belief, morality, and worship. Since then, and down to the present day, all the great catechisms have followed the schematic outline (varying only in sequence) of creed, code, and cult—doctrines of belief, code of ethics, and sacraments of worship.... The *General Directory for Catechesis* is a new champion of Christian faith as a whole way of life. It speaks of the "profound unity of the Christian life" which entails—in old traditional terms—*lex credendi, lex vivendi*, and *lex orandi*—the "law" of belief, of living, and of prayer (#122). It says repeatedly that the "faith demands to be known, celebrated, lived, and translated into prayer—reflecting the sequence of the *Catechism of the Catholic Church*. In another section it refers to 'the contents of catechesis' (note the plural) as 'cognitive, experiential, and behavioral (#35)."" (Groome, p. 15)

If one looks at the current catechism, one sees the four pillars of our faith clearly laid out—creed, sacraments, morality, and prayer. The church remains faithful to these interrelated entities:

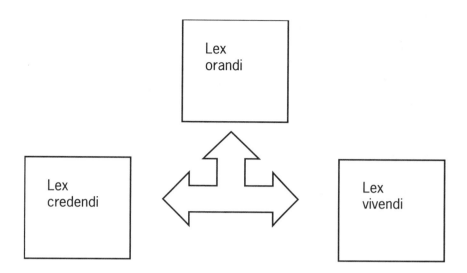

What we do, what we know and value, and how we worship are integrated, inseparable realities. At the heart of event-centered learning is helping participants make the connections between the events of church life that we participate in and the creedal beliefs of Catholicism. There are no acts of worship, community, justice and service, and moral living that stand apart from our beliefs, and there are no beliefs that stand disconnected from our practice. All that we believe is incarnated in the events of faith life. To truly engage in these events, we must both prepare ourselves beforehand and reflect on our experience afterward, allowing the depth and challenge of the event to transform our lives.

The *General Directory for Catechesis* (1997), building on some of the insights from the Second Vatican Council, strongly advocates for an integrated approach to catechesis that weaves together practice, worship, and knowledge. The six fundamental tasks of catechesis defined by this document (GDC #85-86) clearly reinforce the dynamic energy and possibilities of event-centered learning:

1. deepen knowledge of the faith (*credendi*)

2. liturgical education that fosters full, conscious, and active participation in liturgy (*orandi*)

3. moral formation that fosters interior transformation and demonstrates the social consequences of the demands of the gospel (*vivendi*)

4. teach people to pray (*vivendi*)

5. prepare people to live in community (*vivendi*)

6. arouse a sense of mission and prepare people to participate actively in the life and mission of the church (*vivendi*)

Note how the weight of the six tasks lands on *vivendi*, the practicing of one's faith!

The tasks of catechesis as articulated in the GDC boost the momentum toward an integration of liturgy, belief, and practice. They work to assure that the arrows in the illustration (below) of *vivendi*, *credendi*, and *orandi*, depict something true in people's lives: that deepening knowledge leads to full participation in liturgy and the practices of Catholic life; that participation in liturgy leads to a deepening sense of one's beliefs as well as a growing commitment to practicing one's faith in daily life; that the practices of Catholic life lead one to fuller, more meaningful participation in liturgy and a deeper understanding of belief.

Charles Foster put forward the following model of event-centered learning/catechesis:

Preparation for the
church event

Participation in the
church event

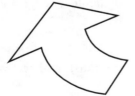

Reflection on the
church event

If we link Foster's model of event-centered learning with the axiom of *vivendi, credendi, orandi*, we can begin to imagine how a community's event-centered, intergenerational curriculum can have at least three different starting points:

1. The curriculum may start with liturgy by *preparing* people for participation in a liturgy. Entry point in Foster's model: preparation for a church event.

- Example: Learners are prepared for the Easter Vigil.

2. The curriculum may start with the experience of liturgy or another church event and guide people to *reflect* on their experience. Through the remembering of what was experienced, and the new awareness and questions that are raised, the learning focus would be on guiding people through an exploration of what beliefs were expressed in the liturgy/event and the implications for one's life. Entry point in Foster's model: reflecting on the event.

- Example: Learners participate in the Easter Vigil then gather to reflect on their experience.

- Example: The learners may participate in a justice practice such as serving the poor, or a cultural celebration such as Black History Month, and reflect on their experience of that event/practice, then explore in more detail the theology of the practice as it connects to the whole of church life.

3. The curriculum may start with some aspect of Catholic belief and guide people through an *exploration* that is intentional about making connections from that doctrine to where it is found in liturgy or other practices. Entry point in Foster's model: preparing for an event.

- Example: The learning community might explore morality—love of God and neighbor—as connected to the Thirtieth Sunday of the lectionary cycle, Year A.

Systematic Catechesis

As evident in the challenges, principles, and guidelines for catechesis in their newest catechetical directory (*National Directory for Catechesis*,

USCCB, 2005), Catholic bishops across the United States are concerned about intentional, systematic, and comprehensive catechesis for all ages. Many Catholic adults are not literate about their faith, and it is feared that many Catholic children are not being systematically catechized in their faith.

With intentionality and clear learning objectives, lifelong systematic catechesis is possible through the event-centered curriculum framework. If *lex orandi*, *lex vivendi*, and *lex credendi* ring true, every event in a parish's faithful expression of church holds within it the doctrinal themes that the bishops are asking all parishes to address.

The events of church life form a spiral curriculum that immerses people more deeply into the faith of the church each year. One need only consider the spiral effect of the three-year liturgical cycle to see how the church seeks to deepen the faith life and practice of its members through liturgical events and through the cycle of lectionary readings. The lifelong faith formation curriculum is formed around the natural rhythm and pattern of the faith community's life as experienced throughout the year. It provides common events and themes that are explored and experienced by all ages and all generations in the faith community.

This lifelong curriculum of church events systematically and comprehensively presents the Gospel message and Catholic tradition through six major content areas that directly correspond to the six tasks of catechesis put forward by the GDC. The six content areas for event-centered learning include: church year feasts and seasons, sacraments, justice and service, morality, prayer and spirituality, and the Creed (see GDC #84-87, 97-115). The *General Directory for Catechesis* (#115) identifies the significance of these major aspects and dimensions of the Christian message for catechesis. The overview (See Appendix One.) presents key paragraphs from the *Directory* that demonstrate the centrality of the six content areas. For example, consider the task of liturgical education that fosters full, conscious, and active participation in liturgy. Approaching that task through the event-centered lens over one year might look like this:

September   Event prepared for: Liturgy of the Eucharist
Learning focus: sacrament of Eucharist,
Liturgy of the Word

October   Event prepared for: Baptism Sunday
          Learning focus: sacrament of Baptism, Part One

November Event prepared for: Advent reconciliation service
          Learning focus: sacrament of Reconciliation

December Event prepared for: Christmas season
          Learning focus: Incarnation and liturgy

January   Event prepared for: International Marriage Day
          Learning focus: sacrament of Marriage

February Event prepared for: Lent
          Learning focus: Transformation through service

March   Event prepared for: Easter Vigil
          Learning focus: sacrament of Baptism, Part Two

April   Event prepared for: celebration of Anointing of the Sick
          Learning focus: Sacrament of the Sick

May   Event prepared for: Pentecost or the parish celebration
          of Confirmation
          Learning focus: sacrament of Confirmation

June   Event prepared for: Corpus Christi
          Learning focus: sacrament of Eucharist,
          Liturgy of Eucharist

The foundational events, already happening in Catholic communal life, contain the theology for a systematic and comprehensive events-centered curriculum. This event-centered approach highlights the Gospel message and Catholic tradition. In fashioning a curriculum, parishes are not limited to these themes and events, rather the event-centered approach encourages parishes to utilize events which come from the life of the parish community itself, its history, its people, and its cultures. For example, a Black Catholic community may prepare its congregation for Black History Month as celebrated in the community, and a Hispanic community may prepare its community for the Feast of Our Lady of Guadalupe. A parish might prepare to celebrate its one-hundredth anniversary by learning about faithfulness and the parish's ongoing call to evangelize the world.

Some events or doctrinal themes rooted in events, are better scheduled at certain points in the liturgical cycle. For example:

- Topics related to Christian morality might be best scheduled during Cycle A, which includes the Great Commandment, Sermon on the Mount, Final Judgment (Matthew 25), and other scripture readings that are intimately linked to Catholic moral teachings.

- Justice doctrine might be best scheduled during Cycle C because so many of the Gospel passages that Catholic social teachings are rooted in are from Luke's Gospel: Rich Man and Lazarus, Good Samaritan.

- Exploring the Creed works well in Cycle A, as many of the doctrinal themes in the Creed relate well to scripture from Cycle A.

- Prayer and sacraments work well with any lectionary cycle as they are the heart of Catholic practice and identity.

Event-centered learning offers a solid and pragmatic approach to systematic catechesis. Again, for a complete guide to events and themes see the *Scope of Church Events and Themes* in Appendix One.

Preparing for an Event: A Reflection Preparation Process

Quite naturally, event-centered intergenerational learning demands faithfulness to what the event or practice has to teach the community. In order to avoid straying from the theology in the actual event, we recommend the following reflection process for leaders responsible for the learning program. This reflection is pragmatic in the manner in which it will draw leaders deeply into the event and challenge them to make activity selections based on the theology rooted in the event. It also provides an opportunity for faith sharing and renewal by breaking open the Word or catholic teaching with one another. The process described below is geared towards a liturgical event, but it can be easily adapted to other events as well. Some adaptations are noted in the text.

Step One In advance, distribute the prayers for the event (for example, in a missal) as well as the readings, and perhaps a brief liturgical commentary. Ask the leaders and planners to read the materials and to jot down the key meanings about the event that surface for them.

> *Adaptation:* If the event is a justice practice, provide a summary of the practice, its history and roots, along with quotes from Catholic social teaching and the Catechism that are connected to the event, as well as scripture connections. If the event is connected to moral teaching, provide Catechism citations, quotes from Catholic moral teachings/documents, and the scripture readings from the Sunday the moral practice is connected to.

Step Two Once everyone has gathered, sing or listen to a simple hymn. Then read one of the prayers and one of the scripture readings from the event, slowly and reflectively.

> *Adaptation:* If the event is a justice or moral practice, read some of the Catechism quotes or relevant scripture readings.

Step Three As a group, quietly ponder what you have just heard in order to receive from it what God wants to give.

Step Four Invite those gathered to share a word or a phrase that has surfaced for them from the prayer/reading/quotes they have just heard.

Step Five Read the prayer/readings/quote again.

Step Six Invite participants to share with the group the insight, challenge, or message they are hearing about the event in the prayer/reading/quotes.

Step Seven Invite prayers of petition from the participants, then close this time of prayer with the Our Father.

Step Eight Spend some time sharing as a group what the most central things are that your parish needs to learn about the event/practice this year. Cluster what surfaces under the areas of:

> *Know What* What theological learning about the event/practice does the parish need? What element/learning theme of systematic catechesis is rooted in this event?

Know How What do we want parishioners to be able to do better this year at this event or because of it: pray, serve others, participate more fully in Eucharist? This is meant to be concrete, guiding learners in explicitly living out their faith.

Know Why What do we want parishioners to better value? What about our Catholic identity are we inviting learners to embrace more fully?

Step Nine Take these insights and ideas to the planning and design of your learning session for the event. *This is the starting point for design!* If there are too many whats, whys, and hows to explore, it is the design team's job to narrow them down and to perhaps integrate some in another learning session.

Celebrating Cultural Gifts

A *parish* is a definite community of the Christian faithful established on a stable basis within a particular church; the pastoral care of the parish is entrusted to a pastor as its own shepherd under the authority of the diocesan bishop. It is the place where all the faithful can be gathered together for the Sunday celebration of the Eucharist. The parish initiates the Christian people into the ordinary expression of the liturgical life: it gathers them together in this celebration; it teaches Christ's saving doctrine; it practices the charity of the Lord in good works and brotherly love. (*Catechism of the Catholic Church*, #2179)

Each parish is an ecclesial community with its own unique character, which means that while remaining faithful to the local bishop and to the universal church, it is called to embody its catholicity in a specific time and place. A Black Catholic community in Washington, DC, celebrates Sunday Eucharist with different traditions—music, gestures, and so on—than a Native American community in southern Arizona, or a white community in Saskatchewan, or a Spanish community in Minnesota. Event-centered learning enables communities to create a curriculum reflective of the unique character of the parish as they seek to provide systematic learning opportunities for their members. It enables them to celebrate the gifts of their culture during faith formation—whether that be a celebration of particular saints, or a secular event with inherent Christian meaning, or other practices that the culture deems important and in sync with Catholic identity.

For example, a rural Native American parish in New Mexico that has been served by Franciscan missionaries for years might choose to prepare for the feast of Saint Francis by providing a learning session about his charisms. The aspects of Saint Francis that they see lived out in their community are justice and service to the poor. A white middle-class parish in suburban United States may also choose to prepare its members for the feast of Saint Francis, but perhaps would focus on their annual tradition of blessing pets and animals on that day. It's the same event but experienced and celebrated differently in each community. The different experience of the event demands a different emphasis in the learning undertaken to prepare the community for it.

Parish cultural events also hold within them gems of Catholic identity and value.

Both the *General Directory for Catechesis* (#109) and the *National Directory for Catechesis* (pp. 64-66) accentuate the need and the challenge of inculturation. Event-centered learning enables parish communities to celebrate their cultural makeup and helps parishioners see Catholic beauty within regular and special events. For example, the Spanish rite of passage for girls, *Quinceañera*, when celebrated in faithfulness to its origins, holds within it a profound respect of virginity and responsibility. The Mass celebrated on that day includes a vow to be a virgin until the day of marriage as well as thanksgiving that the young woman has come of age.

Event-centered learning celebrates the beauty and richness of both the local and univeral church and challenges parish leaders to "penetrate the deepest strata of persons and peoples by the Gospel," bringing the Gospel to events that need to be transformed by it, and celebrating the presence of the Gospel already there.

Being a Eucharistic Community

Have you ever wondered how we will ever be able to fully understand the central event of Eucharist when we live in such a divided world?

We divide believers and non-believers, we segregate young and old, we distinguish between cultures and languages and needs. We manage to creatively divide ourselves at every opportunity.

Yet, our Christian faith challenges us again and again to witness the hope and possibility of community to the world. Through the celebration of Eucharist, we seek to proclaim that all are welcome, all belong, all are united together through the life, death, and resurrection of Jesus Christ. We are called to participate in the events of our faith together: to serve together, to heal together, to pray together, to build community together. We are of one faith, called to be disciples in every moment of our lives. As the *Catechism of the Catholic Church* states:

> In Christian usage, the word 'church' designates the liturgical assembly, but also the local community or the whole universal community of believers. These three meanings are inseparable. 'The church' is the People that God gathers in the whole world. She exists in local communities and is made real as a liturgical, above all, a Eucharistic, assembly. She draws her life from the word and the Body of Christ and so herself becomes Christ's Body. (#752)

If we believe we are the People of God, we need to embrace the call to relationships that being a people demands. Not just relationships of the same, but relationships of the diverse. The young must seek to understand the perspective and stories of their elders. And often the child, in the simple witnessing of her faith, has softened the heart of an elder, enabling the Spirit to enter. The faithful testimony of a young adult has moved adolescents to re-evaluate their priorities and directions. One isn't a "people" alone! One is not formed or fashioned into a people in isolation; it is only in community, through our participation in events, rooted in the grace and power of the Trinity that we can be the People of God.

> In giving attention to the individual, it should not be overlooked that the recipient of catechesis is the whole Christian community and every person in it. If indeed it is from the whole life of the church that catechesis draws its legitimacy and energy, it is also true that "her inner growth and correspondence with God's plan" depend essentially on catechesis. (GDC, #168)

Intergenerational learning provides an opportunity to gather the whole parish to learn, pray, celebrate, and share, while fulfilling expectations for intentional, systematic, and comprehensive faith formation. It has tremendous benefits for the parish and for individuals through its potential to invite all members into full, conscious, and active participation in *all* the events of church life.

End Notes

Congregation for the Clergy. *General Directory for Catechesis.* Washington, DC: USCCB Publishing, 1997.

Foster, Charles. *The Future of Christian Education: Educating Congregations.* Nashville, TN: Abingdon Press, 1994.

Groome, Thomas, and Michael J. Corso, editors. *Empowering Catechetical Leaders.* Washington, DC: NCEA, 1999.

Libreria Editrice Vaticana. 1994. *Catechism of the Catholic Church.* Washington, DC: United States Conference of Catholic Bishops (USCCB).

CHAPTER THREE

Learners and Learning Today

The "Smith" family headed to the soup kitchen for their regular weekly commitment of kitchen cleaning. Each week they scrub the entire kitchen and prepare it for the next week of food preparation and service. Samantha, who lives on the street and is a soup kitchen patron, meets them each week to help out. The Smiths treat Samantha as an equal and accept her for who she is. While returning home the family often talks about Samantha's stories of living on the street, and how those stories challenge them to be good stewards of their own resources...

As the Children's Museum opened, children and adults made their way to the main display areas. One display focused on home heating and the process of insulating a house. Another display showed a variety of bugs and insects; attendees were challenged to match the bug's shape to its name. A third display involved circus props and costumes, and a museum employee helped attendees create a circus show...

The children gathered with their grandparents around the newly purchased "Cranium" game. Grandma was laughing too hard to draw the item that the card indicated and for the rest of the team to guess. The ten-year-old had earlier performed a few lines of Hamlet in the hopes that his team might remember that it came from Shakespeare. Grandpa had earlier tried to help his team see the connections between a collection of three items...

Michael can barely cook but has a whole file on his computer filled with recipes that he hopes to try one day. His favorite TV channel is the food network and he spends perhaps too much time watching expert chefs prepare everything from granola to flaming shrimp kebabs. He is intrigued by the cooking techniques and the combination of foods used to create the final product. He loves to share the recipes with his mom who keeps asking him to watch less and cook more…

Jan and her two daughters were going home from the parish intergenerational learning session that had just finished. As they drove, they laughed together about how Grandma had to keep taking steps backward during the "I'm Sorry" game that they had played to explore sin and contrition. They chatted together about the images of the Holy Spirit and talked about where they were going to hang their windsock when they got home.

What do these stories hold in common? Each is about learning. Learning can be defined as

> the natural process of pursuing personally meaningful goals, and it is active, volitional, and internally mediated; it is a process of discovering and constructing meaning from information and experience, filtered through the learner's unique perceptions, thoughts, and feelings. (*The Power to Transform: Leadership That Brings Learning and Schooling to Life*, Stephanie Pace Marshall, p. 39)

As Christians, our faith in Jesus Christ is a commitment to learning. It is the process of pursuing goals that are connected to the meaning of love and service as witnessed to us by Jesus. Our call to discipleship is a process of discovering the meaning of life and our Christian mission from all the information and experiences that life offers us. Learning is about transformation. Being a disciple of Jesus is about a life of change and metanoia as we seek to practice our lives in faithful witness to the challenge of discipleship. Our personally meaningful goals are connected to growing in a life of faith.

We are disciples in community, and much of our learning happens as we pray, serve, worship, relate, and seek to understand our faith. Learning happens when we use our God-given free will and creativity to "figure" out what something means, to learn a new skill or understand current or new information, or when change forces us to look at things in a new way.

As a faith community we share a *story*, a story that connects us to the conversion (learning!) required for being faithful to our covenant relationship with God, Jesus, and the Holy Spirit. We share the story of creation; we share the story of Moses serving to save the Hebrew people; we share the story of Mary's yes; we share the story of Jesus' life, death, and resurrection. A story or paradigm is "that dominant and potent story that most embodies our worldview and captures our identity, purpose, and sense of belonging. This story shapes our understanding of the past, our perceptions of the present, and our vision for the future" (Marshall, p. 5).

Past, present, and future are not easily discovered, shared, or celebrated when one generation stands separate from another. Our story of learning and change is one that must continually be lived, proclaimed, and understood through the perceptions of learners of all ages.

One great window into community is through the format of intergenerational learning. This gathering of the generations enables the story to be shared and nurtured *from* each generation and *to* each generation. As a community of learners the unique perceptions, thoughts, and feelings of all members are engaged in the journey of faith. Without sharing our story, we soon lose our intimate connection and shared commitment to a common purpose. We lose the hope and joy of learning about the God whom we love and are called into dynamic relationship with.

As Christians, we believe we are called to be the Body of Christ and that through Eucharist we are transformed into that Body. Yet, when it comes to learning and learning formats, we fail to utilize the transformative power of the Body of Christ, the whole community. As Marshall says in her book, "We become the story we tell ourselves about ourselves" (p. 5). One of the stories many churches have been telling themselves for the past fifty years is that adults and children cannot learn together, and teens need to be separated into their own group for learning.

Our experience with and our research into intergenerational learning have convinced us that it is time for the story to change; it is time for the story we tell ourselves to honor the power and potential of the intergenerational learning community. This chapter seeks to lay out the foundational principles and values that enable learners of all ages to fully enter into the process of discovering and constructing meaning.

Bottom line, "deep learning is more likely when a multigenerational community is purposefully learning, exploring, and co-creating together" (Marshall p. 109). It makes sense, then, that the power of learning is increased when all members are impassioned and engaged in the journey of learning; when all are engaged in the common journey of seeking out meaning, purpose, and direction.

Let us look at some of what we know to be true about learners and learning today, and connect that knowledge to the experience of intergenerational learning.

Divine Methodology

An important place to start, before exploring any other principles, is to remind ourselves of divine methodology. The *National Directory for Catechesis* states:

> God's own methodology inspires a plurality of methods in contemporary catechesis. The method or methods chosen, however, must ultimately be determined by a law that is fundamental for the whole of the church's life. Catechetical methodology must exhibit a twofold fidelity. On the one hand, it must be faithful to God and to his Revelation, on the other, it must respect the liberty and promote the active participation of those being catechized. From the beginning of time, God has adapted his message to earthly conditions so that we might be able to receive it. (p. 94)

How is the story we tell through catechesis faithful to God and his revelation when we segment the community to tell it? God's revelation is to all people, and the story of God's revelation must be shared at times through an intergenerational setting that engages all learners in the sharing of their experience, in interacting with Word and tradition, and in challenging one another to respond faithfully. This divine methodology also has a profound and deep respect for the learner. Divine methodology respects that God invites us into a relationship with the Trinity, but clearly points out that learners freely choose to actively participate or not. It seems odd that we as church allow adults to exercise their freedom to learn or not while we force children and teens to learn without inviting their parents to also be accountable in their faith through a commitment to learning.

"The most powerful motivation for learning is meaning and the belief that you can influence the context, conditions, and outcomes of your own learning and your own life. Our children (learners) must believe that they are capable and worthy before they can see their remarkable potential for world shaping" (Marshall, p. 87). Divine methodology is one that empowers the learners to want to learn and to want to make a difference. We believe that intergenerational learning is one context that enables an entire household and intergenerational community to see together how their faith, on God's initiative, has the power in partnership with the Trinity to change the world.

This articulation of divine methodology also makes it very clear that how catechesis is "delivered" must be adapted to earthly conditions so that the learners will be open and able to receive it. It is therefore important that we pay attention to learners and learning theory today, so that we might best be able to create a solid context and methodology for learning.

Principles Common to All Learners

We believe that the principles that follow are universal in nature, and that if we apply them to all learners, each will have a better chance of actually learning what he or she is currently studying.

LEARNING INVOLVES THE WHOLE PERSON

A quick review of the literature on learning and education reveals that whether learners are young or old, effective learning engages the whole person. Good learning engages the heart in imagining what can be, provides opportunities for deepening one's cognitive understanding, and nurtures skills and practices to live one's life in a new way.

Can children, teens, and adults engage in learning at the same time when all are at different levels of cognition, practice, and valuing? Yes, if the methodology enables that to happen. Consider how Jesus reached people of all ages through his parables. How might learners of all ages receive the parable of the fig tree?

Then Jesus told this parable:

> A man had a fig tree planted in his vineyard; and he came looking for fruit on it and found none. So he said to the gardener, "See here! For three years I have come looking for fruit on this fig tree, and still I find none. Cut it down! Why should it be wasting the soil?" He replied, "Sir, let it alone for one more year, until I dig around it and put manure on it. If it bears fruit next year, well and good; but if not, you can cut it down." (Luke 13:6–9)

A five-year-old child hearing this story might find himself thinking, "Yikes. Poor tree. I wonder if the tree got another chance to be a better tree?" A nine-year-old might find herself wondering, "The tree must serve some sort of purpose. I hope it gets another chance, just like I often get when I don't get things right on the first or second try." Teenagers might find themselves thinking, "Maybe the tree doesn't know yet what fruit it is supposed to bear. Good thing that the gardener asked for another year!" Adults might find themselves trying to figure out who the gardener is most like. "Is the gardener the Jesus figure in the story, advocating for the disciple to be given another chance by God? I hope Jesus never gives up advocating for me! I think I need to help others be fruitful disciples too!"

Did this learning through story engage persons of all ages? Yes, definitely. Each learner was able to pull from the story meaning, relevance, and understanding for their lives. "Cognition (learning)…is both biological and social, a dynamic and self-organizing process of constructing meaning by matching new learning to existing patterns and creating new patterns of connections" (Marshall, p. 22). If learning happens through the connection of matching to existing patterns (experience) and creating new patterns, cross generational learning can involve the whole person in effective learning experiences.

EPIC

To summarize Leonard Sweet in his book *Post Modern Pilgrims: First Century Passion for The 21ˢᵗ Century,* learning in today's world has to include experience, participation, images, and connection to others (EPIC). Learners in this computer and mass media era do not want to hear about faith, they want to *experience* faith. They do not want to blindly accept information or formation because an authority tells them to, but rather want to interactively *participate* with the information and seek to use their internal authority to integrate it. Learners in today's world are *image* driven, the oral or print tradition is inadequate without also including images. Lastly, learners in today's world are seeking an experience of *connection*, meaningful relationships with those they are invited to journey with.

Good intergenerational learning provides learners of all ages with an *experience* of faith through prayer, ritual, and story. Learners are invited to *participate* in the learning experience through reading and discussing scripture together, creating a presentation about church, or playing a game that depends on working the challenges out together. Participants are surrounded by *images* of our faith—Bible, candles, banners, take-home craft projects like wind socks and luminaria candle bags. Finally, intergenerational learning intentionally nurtures the *relationships* across the generations, creatively and intentionally nurturing cross-generational relationships.

LEARNING HAS TO BE CONNECTED

The *National Directory for Catechesis* says that

> Catechesis links human experience to the revealed word of God, helping people ascribe Christian meaning to their own existence. It enables people to explore, interpret, and judge their basic experiences in light of the Gospel. Catechesis helps them relate the Christian message to the most profound questions in life: the existence of God, the destiny of the human person, the origin and end of history, the truth about good and evil, the meaning of suffering and death, and so forth. (p. 98)

One of the abilities needed to link human experience to the Christian message is the ability to reflect—the ability to stop, look, and listen to the moment just experienced or about to be experienced. Reflection is almost a lost art in our Christian communities and is an art that needs learning and practicing across the generations if we are to remain connected to our identity as disciples.

Imagine the impact when parents and children gather in a common learning experience and spend time reflecting together on how they have experienced God that day. Imagine the learning that could take place when people of all ages reflect together on the Sunday Gospel and ponder how they are called to live out the message in their daily lives. As Thomas Groome says in his book *Empowering Catechetical Leaders*, "catechesis for the reign of God and a life of Christian faith advises that people's own lives be directly engaged in the catechetical process—as an aspect of the curriculum. Such a holistic faith must be grounded in and return to people's own praxis" (p. 26).

All experience is valid, important, and rich with meaning and connections. It doesn't matter if it is the experience of a four-year-old or a seventy-year-old, God is not confined by the age restrictions we have sought to place on learners in our age-segregated world.

ABILITY TO EFFECT CHANGE

Adult learners are known for their pragmatism. What will I be able to do with this learning? Connected to the pragmatism is the sense of, "what difference will it really make?" Both children and adults and everyone in between want learning to hold within it the power to effect change and to make sense both now and later.

Learners today want to know that what they are expected to learn is relevant in the complexity of relationships and values in their life. They want to know how the learning will enable them to make a difference in the world. Intergenerational learning, like all faith formation offerings, needs to provide a context in which persons of all ages begin to see that with the power and grace of the Holy Spirit the kingdom of God is obtainable.

Imagine children who have been learning about their faith only in an age-segregated schooling model for several years. Each time they leave the catechetical session, they are challenged to go and live their life more fully as disciples of Jesus Christ. They are claimed from the catechism class by a parent or guardian who, for the most part, probably has not spent much time learning about their faith since they themselves were a child. What hope does the child have of effecting change in the household? But imagine how that ability to effect change would increase by having the parent or guardian learning alongside the child!

An intergenerational learning context can also be a great place to remind adults of their power to implement change by providing them with a place to interact with the hope of youth. Adults often say that the hope and enthusiasm of youth help them reclaim their own ability to effect change. Discipleship is about transforming the world, it is about believing that through the power of the Holy Spirit change is possible. Intergenerational learning can be one context that provides for this hope and power to be nurtured so that all generations celebrate and act on their power to make change happen.

MULTIPLE INTELLIGENCES

The theory of multiple intelligences was developed in 1983 by Dr. Howard Gardner, professor of education at Harvard University. It suggests that the traditional notion of intelligence, based on I.Q. testing, is far too limited. Dr. Gardner proposes eight different intelligences to account for a broader range of human potential in children and adults. Respecting these intelligences in an intergenerational context is another way to ensure that learners of all ages are engaged in the learning being offered. The intelligences are not divided by age or developmental stage, but are rather based on innate capacities that cross generations.

- **Linguistic intelligence** involves sensitivity to spoken and written language, the ability to learn languages, and the capacity to use language to accomplish certain goals. This intelligence includes the ability to effectively use language to express oneself rhetorically or poetically and as a means to remember information.
- **Logical-mathematical intelligence** consists of the capacity to analyze problems logically, carry out mathematical operations, and investigate issues scientifically.
- **Musical intelligence** involves skill in the performance, composition, and appreciation of musical patterns.
- **Bodily-kinesthetic intelligence** entails the potential of using one's whole body or parts of the body to solve problems. It is the ability to use mental abilities to coordinate bodily movements.
- **Spatial intelligence** involves the potential to recognize and use the patterns of wide space and more confined areas.

- **Interpersonal intelligence** is concerned with the capacity to understand the intentions, motivations, and desires of other people. It allows people to work effectively with others.
- **Intrapersonal intelligence** entails the capacity to understand oneself, to appreciate one's feelings, fears, and motivations. In Howard Gardner's view it involves having an effective working model of ourselves, and to be able to use such information to regulate our lives.
- **Naturalist intelligence** enables human beings to recognize, categorize and draw upon certain features of the environment. It "combines a description of the core ability with a characterization of the role that many cultures value."

Respecting the multiple intelligences of the learner lends solid support to cross-generational learning. Intelligence is not defined by age or cognitive ability, but by a combination of intelligences and experiences. The multiple intelligences, when well respected in the creation of intergenerational learning experiences, provide adults with new ways to learn that they may not have had in their earlier schooling experiences. Having teens and children in the room gives adults the opportunity to try new ways of learning. For example, for many adults who associate learning only with lectures, learning through designing a home space that nurtures faith when learning about sacraments (spatial intelligence) or using a body sculpture to portray servant leadership (bodily-kinesthetic intelligence), and sharing the learning experience with children and teens, gives them "permission" to participate.

Intergenerational learning allows the faith community to be more creative in the learning experiences that are offered, so that the experience not only crosses generations but also crosses intelligences.

LEARNING HAS CLEAR GOALS

Though programmers and designers sometimes feel stressed by learning outcomes and objectives, learners like to know what they will learn and gain through the learning experience. What will they know by the end of the learning experience? Will they know the why and the values behind the what? How will they be able to live their lives differently because of the learning experience?

In some situations, intergenerational experiences have been simply designed as fun, fluffy events with little attention to achieving any learning goals. Good intergenerational learning raises the bar for what will take place and chooses learning activities accordingly. Clearly articulated learning objectives are critical to ensure that all learners accomplish what needs to be accomplished, while allowing space for the spontaneity of the Holy Spirit to intervene as needed.

Planned and Spontaneous Experience

Learners of all ages feel safe in an environment in which they know what to expect. For example, there is a pattern to the gathering—eat, pray, experience an activity together as a whole group, explore the topic in-depth, and end with prayer. Within the pattern, though, there is space for the spontaneous: a song that just needs to be sung, a story that arises from the community, an adapted learning activity prompted by the nudging of the Holy Spirit.

(Chapter Five explores in more detail the patterns and formats that can be used in the creation of intergenerational learning experiences.)

Learning through Practice

People often learn best by doing. In the Christian tradition we best learn how to pray by praying, we understand the concept of service best by serving others, and we learn how to be in community by living in community. Being a Christian is about practicing what we believe, and learners of all ages learn best when practice is an integral part of their learning experience.

Intergenerational learning provides a venue for learners of all ages to learn by doing together. It also provides a venue for "linking experienced Christian believers with those seeking a deeper relationship between Christ and the church" (NDC, p. 104). In the practice of apprenticeship or mentoring it is not just those being "mentored" who learn, but through the sharing of skills and insights the mentors in turn find themselves learning about their skills. The mentoring is not always adult to child, but may also be a child to adult.

LEARNING THROUGH WITNESS

The *National Directory for Catechesis* says that "catechesis for prayer begins when children see and hear others praying" (p. 113). There is no doubt that the witness and story of others, when paid attention to, has the power to help us learn.

Consider the following story told at an intergenerational learning session addressing the topic of death and resurrection. Organizers sought a real life story to engage participants in the concrete meaning of death and resurrection.

An older woman told the story of her son's tragic death in a car accident. She spoke of how hard it was for her in the first few months after her son's death, how she did not know how she was going to be able to continue living without him. Her pain was great, and each day she said she would ask God to please help her deal with the pain. Some days she said she was so angry with God for taking her son that she yelled at God and demanded of God to explain to her why her son had died. The months passed but the pain didn't go away. It dimmed a little, but the absence of her son was felt especially when her family gathered for birthdays or special family events. One day the mother received a letter from the other driver in the accident, seeking forgiveness for his role in her son's death, and pledging to keep living his life as though every minute was gift, as though he too could die at any time like her son had. The other driver shared how his life had been transformed through his attitude of seeing each moment as gift, and now his relationships with family and others took much greater precedence over work or making a fortune.

The room was silent while the mother spoke. Even the young children knew the story was too important to miss. As the participants gathered in pairs to share what they had learned about death and resurrection in the woman's story, learners of all ages grasped anew the meaning of Jesus' death and resurrection.

Witness and story have the power to grab the heart and open the mind to new ways of looking at the world and practicing one's faith. As Barbara L. McCombs says so eloquently in her book *What Do We Know about Learners and Learning*, "personal change in one's perceptions, values, attitudes and beliefs results from transformations in thinking. These transformations in thinking most often result from critical connections made in one's own understanding, knowledge, and ways of thinking, as well as from critical connections—personal relationships—with others of significance in the learning environment" (p. 192).

BOTH TEACHER AND LEARNER

The *National Directory for Catechesis* also states that "every individual has the responsibility to grow in faith and to contribute to the growth in faith of the other members of the church" (p. 186). Later the NDC says that "All members…participate in the church's catechetical mission" (p. 217).

One parish community in Colorado invited the entire faith community to stand up and be commissioned as catechists on the USCCB's National Catechetical Sunday in order to challenge the community to see that all were called to teach and to learn.

In an intergenerational learning context, it is critical that adults are not there just to teach the children but to allow the children to be teaching them as well. Perhaps children are not playing a formal catechetical role but they are catechizing, as are teens, through their witness, presence, stories, insights, and questions.

HOSPITABLE AND COMFORTABLE SPACE

It's hard to learn in a space that feels cold and distant, where participants are not called by name, where everyone sits in their little groups and new participants feel excluded. It's hard to learn when the chairs are hard, the tables are long and wide so you cannot hear anyone, or when participants are cramped into a tight space.

Young or old, intergenerational learning works best in a hospitable and comfortable physical setting. Parishes that do hospitality well often cite the following practices:

- Participants are warmly welcomed by hospitality ministers.
- No one or no household is left sitting alone—someone from the team either joins them or introduces them to others.
- Furniture is friendly for all ages—there are high chairs or booster seats for little children, the seniors with walkers have adequate space to move around, and so on.
- Time is taken for community building and intentionally getting to know one another in a safe and fun way.

- Participants are challenged to take care of one another by taking turns at being the table prayer leader, table clearer, and table supply "getter."

What about Developmental Stages?

The process of growing, maturing, and becoming fully alive is a graced, predictable, yet mysterious process. Intergenerational learning can be a nurturing place for learners of all ages to help each other grow and unfold as persons move through the developmental stages of life. In her book *Human Development and Faith*, Felicity Kelcourse makes this point:

> Development is not only linear. It is an organic unfolding, similar to the process shown in slow-motion films of the growth of flowers. Growth occurs not in single directions, but outward, like the concentric rings of a tree trunk. Plants and trees do not only grow up, but toward all their sources of energy. They reach up toward the light, outward into the air, and downward into their source of nourishment. Trees also build structure as they grow—over the years, layers are added to the trunk, building a structure of support, storage of nutrients, and an outer layer of bark that protects the tree against the buffeting realities of wind, fire, and the axe. This is a much more adequate and organic metaphor for human psychological development than a linear model. (p. 93)

Some adult educators who have never experienced the learning power of an intergenerational community believe that learning and development are only possible in developmentally respective, age-specific contexts. They close themselves off from a phenomenal opportunity for adult faith growth and development because they believe adults and children are incapable of learning in the same context together. Are there times when adults need to learn just with other adults? Most definitely, especially when the topic warrants it—just as it is important for children and teens to have opportunities to learn with their peers. Is it necessary that adults always learn just with other adults? Definitely not.

Consider the grandmother who is taught how to use her computer by her teenage grandson. Consider the learning experience of the elder generation when they are partnered with grade-one students and spend time reading books together. Consider the middle-aged man who learns how to rock climb with his children. Consider the aunt and uncle whose visiting niece or nephew teaches them how to recycle. We learn intergenerationally in non-intentional ways all the time.

Since we are talking about learning about one's faith, it makes sense to spend some time exploring one theory of faith development and see how intergenerational learning is one of several healthy means to nurture faith development for all ages and stages. In his book *Will Our Children Have Faith* John Westerhoff articulates four phases of faith development, that is, how people arrive at personal faith in God.

Westerhoff's first phase is *affective*. He states that people first come to believe in God by experiencing the unconditional love of another. Basically, I am able to believe that God loves me because I have experienced the love, affection, and attention of another. In Westerhoff's articulation, most children are at this stage of faith development. In today's world we also know of many teens and adults who have not been loved or nurtured by significant others and who struggle to experience the love of God as they wrestle with the affective phase of faith development.

The second phase is *affiliative*. We continue to grow in our faith by participating in the rituals and stories of a community of faith. I may not have obtained ownership of my own faith, but I have a sense of the importance and power of faith because I am affiliated with a believing community. Westerhoff says that early adolescents are often in this phase. Have you ever asked a young teen why they go to church? The most common response: "because my parents and family go to church." Again, there are many adults and older youth who would say the same thing, who have not owned their communal membership yet, but are strengthened in their faith through the witness of other believers around them.

Westerhoff points out that once people move through a phase of faith, they may experience it again. For example, often when people experience crisis and are angry at God or experience disillusionment with the faith community, they may find themselves unable to believe in God in their heart of hearts but are strengthened to keep believing through the steadfast faith and witness of others around them.

The third phase is *searching*. The "seeker" questions and probes all that they have known and believed, in order to achieve their own answers and to be able to believe in God. Seeker strive to have faith, not because others around them believe, but because in their seeking they want to personally know God's meaning and significance in their lives. How many of us as adults find ourselves seeking and searching to find meaning and purpose in our own lives? How many of us experience trials and tribulations and seek to make sense of them and of our faith in God?

The fourth phase is *owned*. Once a "seeker" has pushed and shoved and questioned all that they know to be true and learned all that is important at the time, they will arrive at a crossroads. The crossroads will be the ability to say or not to say, "I'm a believer. I know and love God and know that my life would not be the same without God in it. I believe and will seek to live out my faith in personal and interpersonal ways."

Let's apply this theory to intergenerational faith formation. How do persons in all four stages benefit from witnessing the faith growth and learning of others at each of the other stages?

Imagine a child or another person of any age who is at the *affective* phase of faith. Affective-phase learners become part of a welcoming, hospitable intergenerational learning community who know them by name, who invest time and energy in building a relationship with them, and the learners come to know God better through the community that relates lovingly with them. They seem to pay little attention to the hard questions sometimes asked, but simply enjoy learning and sharing with people of all ages.

Imagine a young adolescent who claims to believe because those around him believe (*affiliative* faith). He comes to the intergenerational learning session with his family or with a peer and is accepted as a contributing member of the community. He undertakes leadership roles; he has opportunities for discussion and learning with both his peers and with adults; and he is immersed into the signs, symbols, stories, and rituals of the faith community. He hears others' faith stories and of the importance of faith and community in their lives. He marvels at a child's simple belief in the resurrection, hears an older teen or adult asking questions to make sense of their experiences, and he is assured of the possibility of faith by the older adults who have experienced many of life's challenges and hard questions—and yet still believe.

Imagine an older teen or young adult who has questions and challenges for the community. She hears others, including adults, asking questions about their faith and has seen how the catechetical leaders do not feel threatened by the questions. Nurtured in this safe and welcoming environment, she too finds her voice and shares her own questions and doubts. No one judges her by her questions but others enjoy her seeking, even if at times the answers are not close at hand. She too marvels at the simple faith the children seem to have and admires the young adolescents for their participation as she remembers her own tensions about belonging to the community. She is challenged by the witness of others who seem to have integrated their questions and doubts as part of their journey in faith. She is comforted with the reality of journey, that there doesn't seem to be an arrival point that she needs to achieve! She challenges the adults in the room for whom faith is taken for granted.

Imagine adults who have moved to own their lives and their faith as disciples. They are challenged to keep learning and deepening their faith through the questions of the "seekers" and are energized by the hope and realness the children bring to the intergenerational learning community. They are pushed to express themselves when the *affiliative* believers seem to engage so simply in symbols and rituals.

Conclusion

How one is asked to "learn" matters profoundly. The how of learning is as important as the content. If we are ever to achieve and nurture lifelong learning in our faith communities, we need to nurture and model to all members a life-giving environment that recognizes the best processes, principles, and structures of learning. Interdependence is vital to the principles of learning. It is an interdependency that is intergenerational. We need to nurture a model of learning that understands faith growth as a continuous and natural process of seeking meaning and purpose as disciples of Jesus Christ.

We are the community of Jesus Christ, a community inspired and challenged to learn, to change, to grow. Intergenerational learning must be a vital part of the community.

End Notes

Groome, Thomas, and Michael J. Corso, editors. *Empowering Catechetical Leaders*. Washington, DC:NCEA, 1999.

Kelcourse, Felicity B. Human *Development and Faith: Life Cycle Stages of Body, Mind, and Soul*. St. Louis, Missouri: Chalice Press, 2004.

Marshall, Stephanie Pace. *The Power to Transform: Leadership that Brings Learning and Schooling to Life*. San Francisco, California: John Wiley & Sons Inc., 2006.

McCombs, Barbara L. *What Do We Know about Learners and Learning? The Learner-Centered Framework: Bringing the Educational System into Balance*. Educational Horizons, Spring 2001.

Smith, M.K. (2002) "Howard Gardner and multiple intelligences," *the encyclopedia of informal education*, http://www.infed.org/thinkers/gardner.htm. Last updated: January 28, 2005.

Sweet, Leonard. *Post-Modern Pilgrims: First Century Passion for the 21st Century World*. Nashville, Tennessee: Broadman and Holman, 2000.

United States Conference of Catholic Bishops. *National Directory for Catechesis*. Washington, DC: USCCB, 2005.

Westerhoff, John. *Will Our Children Have Faith?* New York: Seabury Press, 1976.

CHAPTER FOUR

Integrated Catechesis

The predominant structures, methods, and practices of catechesis in the U.S. Catholic Church today are not supported by what the church actually says about catechesis.

You will not find church documents that tell you that formal parish faith formation must occur on a weekly basis. You will not find church documents that tell you to conduct all faith formation in a school-type classroom. You will not find church documents that tell you that ALL faith formation must be age-specific and "developmentally appropriate." You surely won't find church documents that tell you that children deserve more of our faith formation efforts and resources than all other age groups. And you won't find church documents that tell you that you must separate and isolate your formal catechetical efforts from most if not all other aspects of ecclesial life.

In this chapter we will present the argument that intergenerational faith formation is one of the key methods for assisting the parish community in effectively fulfilling its catechetical responsibilities. It's not the only method or setting, but it is one that is more compatible with the church's vision of catechesis than the school-house model. Also, it is a method, that, when employed well, also lends credence to the niche that age-specific faith formation has a clear role to play—but not the only role.

After quickly reviewing the overall aim of catechesis, this chapter will make a case for intergenerational faith formation by recognizing that:

- Catechesis is rooted in community life, and intergenerational catechesis best mirrors the life of the community.
- Faith formation is lifelong, and intergenerational catechesis provides an ideal "entry point" for all ages—peewee to oldster—to embark upon or continue their journey of faith growth.
- Catechesis must be integrated with all aspects of parish life, and intergenerational faith formation provides an ideal foundation for doing this.
- Catechesis becomes effective only when faith formation continues at home, and intergenerational faith formation provides the best platform to model in a gathered setting what must take place in the home setting.

Aim of Catechesis

What is the aim of catechesis? Several references to key church documents provide helpful insights:

> It is a proper and grave duty especially of pastors of souls to take care of the catechesis of the Christian people so that the living faith of the faithful becomes manifest and active through doctrinal instruction and the experience of Christian life. (Canon 773)

> The aim of catechetical activity consists in precisely this: to encourage a living, explicit, and fruitful profession of faith. (GDC, #66)

> The definitive aim of catechesis is to put people not only in touch, but also in communion and intimacy, with Jesus Christ. (GDC, #80)

> [Catechesis] is a form of the ministry of the word, which proclaims and teaches. It leads to and flows from the ministry of worship, which sanctifies through prayer and sacrament. It supports the ministry of service, which is linked to efforts to achieve social justice and has traditionally been expressed in spiritual and corporal works of mercy. (*To Teach as Jesus Did*, #32)

Take a moment and go back. Read each of the four quotes slowly and carefully. As you can see, catechesis is *not* something the church does just because we've always done it. It has a purpose that is *essential* to both the individual's pursuit of grace and salvation and to the overall mission of the church.

At the very beginning of her book *Fashion Me a People,* Maria Harris described the aim of catechesis well by stating that we are a people with a pastoral vocation, and with it comes responsibilities.

> No longer is it enough to be passive members, receiving a word told us by someone else, filing that word away to be taken out for a reading now and then…. We are realizing that the word of God is addressing us, saying something to us, making demands on us, and asking us to live that word in our lives. We are a people called by the gospel, called to make a difference in the world. (p. 24)

The reason we receive catechesis is to fulfill our pastoral vocation to make a difference in the world. This implies a particular way of living, that is, in communion and intimacy with Jesus Christ.

We can say with confidence that the fundamental tasks of catechesis are to proclaim Christ's message, to journey with others to faithful communion and intimacy with Christ, to participate in efforts to develop community, to lead people to worship and prayer, and to motivate them to serve others.

It's the Community

In your parish who catechizes? Your parish likely has designated leaders who facilitate faith formation for children, youth, and adults. Yes, these people catechize. Your parish likely convenes small groups for faith sharing, scripture study, and the like. Yes, those who lead and participate in these groups catechize one another. Your parish likely participates in service and outreach to those in need. Yes, the leaders of these efforts engage in catechesis. Your parish likely sponsors community events to bring people together, and it just may be that the leaders or your pastor may catechize in this context. And certainly your parish worships each Sunday, and the homily breaking open the Word of God involves catechesis.

The *General Directory for Catechesis* has a very clear idea about who catechizes.

> Catechesis is nothing other than the process of transmitting the Gospel, as the Christian community has received it, understands it, celebrates it, lives it, and communicates it in many ways. (GDC, #105)

> These are the profound reasons for which the Christian community is in herself living catechesis. Thus she proclaims, celebrates, works, and remains a vital, indispensable, and primary *locus* of catechesis. (GDC, #141)

With this in mind, we can say that all those leaders mentioned in the previous paragraph participate with and contribute to the catechesis of the *community*. It is through the whole life of the community that catechesis occurs, and this is more than just an ideal vision statement. It is a point of fact. For good or ill, catechesis is affected by and facilitated through the life of the community. The deliberate, programmatic efforts of "formal" catechesis are in effect "supplemental" (though not optional) to the broad, foundational catechetical power of the whole community.

Without healthy, holy, and relational community, a parish's programmed catechetical efforts will likely fall flat. Whereas, if the life of the community is vibrant and strongly rooted in faith, even mediocre catechetical programs will yield positive outcomes. For good or ill, it's the community that catechizes.

It is also the community of the home that catechizes. Familiar to many is the well worn statement: "Parents are the primary educators in the faith" (GDC, #255). This is simply a point of fact. For good or ill, for positive or negative, parents have the first and most faith influence on their children. What if we, as catechetical leaders, truly believed that? Would we spend so much time, energy, and resources on children, and comparatively so much less on the adults who actually have such influence? Can we invest in parental education and formation as much as we invest in catechist certification programs? Can we begin to see every contact that we have with parents as an opportunity for evangelization and faith formation?

The best thing a parish can do for its catechetical programs is become a more authentic community of faith.

We believe intergenerational faith formation programming is one way to do that. Why not come together to learn in the same way we come together to worship—everyone all together? The true nature of the community is best revealed and represented in its worship. But this nature can also be mimicked in its learning format. Bring all the generations together, lead them through a deliberate, well-conceived, and organized lesson plan, and watch the faith learning blossom!

Intergenerational learning also mirrors the community. Instead of segmenting individuals into like age groups, we let them experience and witness the learning that takes place among all ages around them. When a middle-schooler sees that a young adult is genuinely learning and growing in his faith, this provides a powerful witness to the young adolescent. Similarly, when a middle-aged adult sees a youngster have an "aha" moment of faith, it freshens and enlivens the faith of the mature adult. When the whole community learns the same thing at the same time, it strengthens the sacred nature of the whole community.

The communal nature of Christian faith means that catechesis has the purpose of nurturing people in ecclesial identity—as people of the church. How are we able to nurture others into this corporate identity when we separate the community from each other by offering only age-specific learning? How do we nurture this ecclesial identity without ever journeying together to explore our experience of God, to critically examine how we are living as people in sync with God's Word?

The Home Community Catechizes

The home community is a critical place of catechesis. Our catechetical effort on the parish campus will simply not have lasting impact unless it is reinforced at home. This is true for children, adolescents, *and* adults. Families and individuals grow in faith when their home life is permeated with faith-based activities, such as faith conversations, rituals and devotions, outreach and service to others. Families engage in these activities when they can be easily woven into the ordinary (and sometimes extraordinary) moments of their daily lives: exits and entries, car time, meal time, bed time, and memory-making time. Families and are more willing and more likely to engage in intentional faith-building activities when they have learned how to recognize the spiritual and faith potential of their own "moments of meaning." In other words, when families have learned the simple art of reflecting on their ordinary lives together to discover God's gracious presence in the creases and folds, they become more intentional about growing in faith at home.

Intergenerational learning provides an ideal context for families and individuals to see how home faith growth can be modeled and shown to them. If we want households to pray at home, we show them how to pray together and invite them to practice praying together in the intergenerational learning context. If we want them to live out their vocation to be people of justice and service, we help them reflect on that together in the intergenerational context, and we challenge them to create a plan of service for which they will be accountable to one another.

If we want families to practice their faith at home, we know that some things are crucial. This much we know:

- We must give them all necessary materials with directions for even the simplest home activity.
- We must package it in a creative way. Anything on 8½" by 11" paper smacks of school and homework, is flat, and gets lost.
- We must make it ready to use, that is, plug 'n' play.
- If they build it, they will use it.
- We must feed them.
- We need to model how it's done in the gathered setting.
- We need to keep it simple.
- We need to use appropriate technology, if only to show we're not totally outdated.

While surely you could add to this list, what it demonstrates is the simple fact that all these things are much more easily done in an intergenerational learning setting than in the traditional age-segmented classroom. With several people from the same household attending, the intergenerational setting simply and profoundly increases the odds that the message will reverberate in the home through discussion, action, and simply carrying out the practices of one's faith.

Faith Formation Is Lifelong

Faith formation is lifelong. This is another "point of *fact*." The journey of faith growth lasts for the whole of life. Again, as parish leaders, if we *really* believed this, would we continue to create formal faith formation programs that by their format and structure imply finishing, graduation? Don't we lament that the celebration of the sacrament of confirmation has become a great rite of exodus from the Catholic Church?

Faith formation is lifelong. This is not a visionary statement. It is simply truth. The problem is that the structures, programs, and ministries of parish life have not adequately supported this truth. We've put so much energy into children—perhaps that's because we have more control over them—and not nearly enough energy into all other stages of life.

Faith formation is lifelong. "This is too obvious to bear repetition, too obvious until we begin to see how major are the revisions this belief demands in our educational curriculum" (Harris, p. 38). Once again we are confronted with the challenge to change our deep-seated patterns of behavior and the various structures we have erected to support that behavior. What if *lifelong* faith formation was our *starting point*? Would we continue to use leftover time, energy, and resources on adults and families? Would we continue to be hyper-concerned about covering an arbitrarily determined amount of doctrinal content at each grade level in order to declare our catechetical efforts "comprehensive and intentional"?

Faith formation is lifelong. "For a people called by the gospel in baptism and confirmation, there is no time in our life when that call ends. Our education into it is ongoing and ought to become increasingly richer and more complex as we develop through adulthood" (Harris, p. 38). The personal journey of one's faith formation continues throughout life, but in most communities the formal support through education is spotty at best after the years of childhood and early adolescence.

What has lifelong faith formation to do with intergenerational learning? Our experience with many parishes in the *Generations of Faith* project shows that intergenerational learning creates an atmosphere of trust and openness that draws and beckons people to learn. It makes learning fun—for all ages—but particularly for adults! We do not deny the problem of religious literacy among many of today's adult generation. We are well aware of the limited success of the religious education process and approach for many of the baby boom generation. The result is that we have many Catholic adults who simply do not know what they think they ought to know about their Catholic faith. But of course, like you and me, they are reluctant to let on what they don't know, unless it is truly safe and supportive to do so and the intergenerational learning context gives them that safe place.

The reality is that the current emphasis for faith formation in the United States and Canada continues to remain focused on children despite many documents like the GDC, NDC, and *Our Hearts Were Burning within Us* (USCCB) calling us to focus on adults and lifelong learning. One of the best ways to reach parents (adults) is through their children. Many of us as parents will do things for our children that we seem unable to find time to do for ourselves. The intergenerational learning context pushes parents to invest time in their own faith formation through the requirement of attending with their children.

One of the pleasant surprises that emerged from our research with *Generations of Faith* parishes is the energy and enthusiasm for learning shown by adults, many of whom are beyond the childrearing years. Essentially, we have found that the intergenerational learning model creates an atmosphere of trust and safety for adults and people of all ages.

As the GDC says so beautifully, "adhering to Jesus Christ, in fact, sets in motion a process of continuing conversion which lasts through the whole of life" (#56). Our challenge as educators is to nurture a faith-formation context, including that of the intergenerational learning experience, that models ongoing learning for all members and which deepens that adherence to Jesus Christ. If the intergenerational learning provided is engaging and on target, learners of all ages will come to see how lifelong the conversion process is. The intergenerational learning context can also be seen as a launch pad for smaller learning experiences, such as small faith-sharing communities, retreats, family-camp experiences, Bible study, and so on.

QUALITATIVE RESEARCH FINDINGS

As mentioned in the Introduction, in the spring of 2005 we conducted qualitative research with parish leaders involved in *Generations of Faith* from nine dioceses around the country. These leaders participated in focus group interviews and in-depth interviews. Participants in the study represented 83 parishes. For more details on the study, see Appendix Two.

Based on direct quotes from parish leaders as they described the impact of intergenerational learning as one of the key methods of faith formation, we arrived at the following "findings." Each of these findings is supported and corroborated by a preponderance of opinions by leaders who participated in the study.

1. There is involvement of all ages and generations—parents and children, teens, young adults, adults, older adults, and whole families—in faith formation through intergenerational learning. It is still a challenge to involve certain groups in the parish, such as Catholic school families, young adults, and single adults.

2. Intergenerational relationships are created as people of all ages learn from one another and grow in faith together.

3. Intergenerational learning strengthened the parish community— through relationship-building and participation in church life. People take time to talk and share.

4. Participation in intergenerational learning led to greater involvement in parish life, including the liturgical and sacramental life of the parish, justice and service projects, and parish ministries.

5. Intergenerational learning addresses a hunger that adults have to learn more about their faith and fill in the gaps in their formation. More adults are participating in faith formation.

6. Families enjoy opportunities to pray, learn, and be together. Families are growing in the ways that they share faith.

7. Intergenerational learning creates an environment in which participants feel safe to learn, ask questions, and grow in faith on a deeper level.

8. Participants are engaged in a variety of learning activities that are experiential, multi-sensory, and interactive. Faith sharing and personal experience are an important element of learning.

9. Adequate parish meeting space plays a key role in conducting successful intergenerational learning programs.

10. Intergenerational learning is exciting—the enthusiasm, joy, and energy are attractive and contagious.

11. Some GOF parishes are succeeding in their efforts to have parents learn alongside their children, while parents in other parishes express a preference for "adult only" learning.

QUANTITATIVE RESEARCH FINDINGS

After articulating the findings from the qualitative research interviews, we then used those findings to conduct quantitative research, inviting all GOF practitioners to indicate their level of agreement or disagreement with the findings. For more details on the quantitative research, see Appendix Two.

With respect to intergenerational learning, GOF practitioners were asked the following question: "The following statements describe the impact of GOF on a parish community and its leaders. Please indicate your parish's degree of agreement with each statement."

(Rating: 1 = strongly disagree, 5 = strongly agree)

4.26 Intergenerational learning engages participants in a variety of learning activities that are experiential, multi-sensory, interactive, and involve faith sharing.

4.06 Families benefit from intergenerational learning through opportunities to pray, learn, and be together. Families are growing in ways that they share faith.

4.0 Intergenerational learning strengthens the parish community through relationship-building and participation in parish life; people take time to talk and share with each other.

3.98 Intergenerational learning provides an environment in which participants feel safe to learn, ask questions, and grow in faith on a deeper level.

3.97 Intergenerational learning addresses a hunger that adults have to learn more about their faith.

3.76 Our parish is reaching new audiences, such as adults and whole families, through intergenerational learning.

3.73   Intergenerational relationships are created through intergenerational learning, as people of all ages learn from each other and grow in faith together.

3.57   There has been an increase in the number of adults participating in faith formation because of intergenerational learning.

We believe that our research is conclusive in showing that intergenerational faith formation, as a format and method, strongly supports the reality that faith formation is lifelong. It's an attractive learning environment for adults as well as young people, and it "provides an environment in which participants feel safe to learn, ask questions, and grow in faith on a deeper level."

Integrated Catechesis

If catechesis is rooted in the life of the community and is lifelong, then of course it must be integrated into all aspects of parish life. As the community lives, moves, and experiences its being, so too it teaches. Learning cannot take place in a vacuum. The content of our faith requires traction in order to take hold in our lives. Our communal experiences of worship, service, prayer, and gathering provide such ecclesial traction. Add to this one's personal and familial experiences of faith and spirituality, and the potential for faith growth and learning skyrockets.

In a classroom model, isolated from the central events of parish life, surrounded by peers of the same age, it's extremely difficult to find the necessary traction for the Jesus story to take hold in a person's life—whether child, teen, or adult. Even if the child, teen, or adult is engaged in the worship and other activities of the parish, if the religious education program runs on its own course in isolation from those other activities, the "student" will likely not make much of a connection between the two, particularly if the student is a child or teen.

Recognizing Christ at the very center of one's spiritual encounter, lifelong faith formation must become an integrated process incorporating 1) formation through participation in the life of the faith community, 2) education in scripture and the Catholic tradition, 3) apprenticeship in the Christian life, 4) knowledge of and intimate connection with the liturgy and rituals of the church, 5) developing of a life of prayer, 6) moral formation in Jesus Christ, and 7) engagement in actions of justice and service.

The last paragraph of the Introduction in the *National Directory for Catechesis* offers a vision of full integration for catechesis and those involved in catechetical ministry.

> The spirituality of those involved in the catechetical ministry centers on an encounter with Christ. It is rooted in the living Word of God. It fosters an abiding hope that all should come to the knowledge of the truth of Christ and accept salvation from him. It expresses itself in a sincere love for the church in imitation of Christ. It seeks interior growth in the peace and joy of Christ. It embraces the Paschal Mystery, enters into the apostolic mission of Christ, and is enriched by a deep devotion to the Mother of God. The challenge to all those involved in catechesis is to bear each of these marks within their hearts and souls. (NDC, #20)

Effective integrated catechesis yields fully integrated Christians, people who grow into a working understanding of and comfort with all aspects of the Christian life: proclaiming the word, service to others, living in community with people of all ages and diversity, praying and worshipping, and teaching others about the faith.

While strict age-segmented, school-house models of catechesis create barriers to integration, intergenerational faith formation both models and delivers integrated catechesis. Particularly if the intergenerational learning is designed to be a preparation program for a forthcoming event in church life, the learning itself leads people out of the "classroom" directly into the life of the community. For example, if the intergenerational learning program is focused on preparing learners to understand the Easter Vigil, the learners are led directly to the Easter Vigil that follows the learning session a week or two later. The learning has direct and immediate application for all. Even the very young can make the connection between learning and doing, when, for example, an intergenerational session on Pentecost is followed by the actual celebration of Pentecost, or when an intergenerational session on one of the principles of Catholic social teaching is followed directly by a communal project of outreach and service.

Also, intergenerational learning itself models integration. By engaging all of the generations in learning together, it provides a catechetical model that gathers the whole parish to learn, build community, share faith, pray, celebrate, and practice their faith. It provides a setting for each generation to share and learn from the other generations. It involves the whole family in learning together and equips families with knowledge, skills, and faith-sharing activities for nurturing faith at home.

An intergenerational program, explored in great detail in Chapter Five, includes five key elements taught in a two-to-three hour timeframe.

1. Gathering and Opening Prayer

2. All-Ages Learning Experience. Intergenerational learning begins with a multigenerational experience of the theme that all the generations share together.

3. In-Depth Learning Experience. Through structured learning activities each generation: families with children, adolescents, and adults explore the meaning of the church event and develop the ability to participate meaningfully in the event. In-depth learning experiences are conducted in different formats:

    • The *Age Group Format* provides parallel, age-appropriate learning for groups at the same time. Though age groups are separated, each one is focusing on the same topic, using specific learning activities that are designed for each life-cycle stage: families with children, adolescents, young adults, and adults.

    • The *Whole Group Format* provides a series of facilitated learning activities for everyone at the same time using intergenerational or age-specific small groups or table groups.

    • The *Learning Activity Center Format* provides structured intergenerational and age-specific learning activities at a variety of stations or centers in a common area.

4. Sharing Learning Reflections and Home Application. In intergenerational groups participants share what they learned and prepare for applying their learning to daily life using the Home Kit.

5. Closing Prayer Service

Conclusion

Intergenerational catechesis offers a great opportunity for a parish or congregation to root catechesis in communal life, to nurture and model lifelong learning, to integrate catechesis with all aspects of parish life, especially through event-centered learning, and to support the home community to be all that it can be.

Parishes across the country are realizing its potential. The following chapter explores in more detail the processes and practices of effective, faith-full, intergenerational learning.

CHAPTER FIVE

The Current Practice of Intergenerational Faith Formation

Intergenerational learning is not a new catechetical format in the Catholic church. Some parishes have been doing some form of it since the early 1980s. Now, however, particularly in the United States, there has never been such a large number of parishes integrating the intergenerational learning format. The Center for Ministry Development alone has trained over fifteen hundred parishes in the methodology, and many other parishes have learned on their own or through other means.

Intergenerational learning might best be viewed as a choreographed dance, incorporating pre-determined steps and movements, while also allowing the gathered community to influence the particular expression of the dance, its tempo and pace, and sometimes even adding a few creative steps along the way. This chapter will explore in some detail a central template for intergenerational learning, the "pre-determined dance steps" so to speak, while offering the reader "best practices" to help the steps respond to the tempo of those gathered.

Let the music begin!

Basic Learning Format

We have identified ten distinct components to the intergenerational learning format. As in any learning template, it is helpful to remember that the components are not separate stand-alone entities, but rather interlocking pieces of a puzzle that intimately link to one another. The learning objectives are recycled, reinforced, and built upon from one component to the next—the "music" of the learning objectives is felt throughout the entire learning experience.

The basic learning format for intergenerational learning includes the following components:

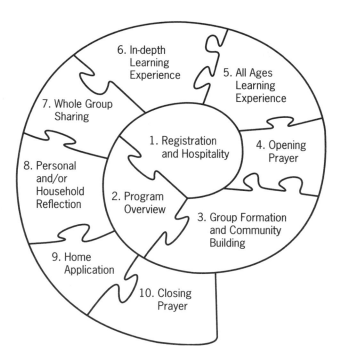

Registration and Hospitality Registration may be needed before the learning event takes place in order to determine the number of people who plan on attending. Registration may also be needed as the learners gather for the session to distribute nametags, handouts, home kits, and perhaps collect outstanding fees. Many parishes start their learning experiences with a snack or meal. Registration is all the more important if a meal is part of the program.

Hospitality is critical toward creating a vibrant learning community. If learners are welcomed warmly, they will more readily participate in the learning program. People learn best in an environment characterized by trust, acceptance, and inquiry. Beyond the gathering, hospitality is critical throughout the entire intergenerational learning experience.

Program Overview People of all ages like to know how they are going to be spending their time together. As the session begins, the learners are given an overview of the program. The agenda is posted on flip chart sheets, PowerPoint slide, or small pocket-sized pieces of paper for individual learners to carry with them.

Group Formation and Community Building In order for the learning to take place, depending on the learning model or activities chosen, learners are divided into learning groups: family clusters, intergenerational groups, or age-specific groups. The grouping choices depend on the learning topic, the physical space, the leadership available, and the number of participants. Community building helps participants feel safe, comfortable, and welcome in the gathering.

Opening Prayer Prayer is an essential part of each learning session and launches the participants into the focus of the session through scripture, ritual, symbols, gesture, and music.

All-Ages Learning Experience The All-Ages Learning Experience provides participants with a common experience to engage them in the topic of the session. A variety of methods can be used in this opening learning experience: drama, simulations, games, storytelling, and so on.

In-depth Learning Experience Generally there are three primary learning formats for the in-depth learning experience: *whole group, age group,* and *learning activity centers*. Learning formats are selected according to audience, facilitation, physical space, and topic.

The *whole group* format gathers all participants into one large space and guides them through each learning experience at the same time.

Imagine a large parish hall or adaptable worship space in which tables—preferably round—and chairs have been set up and people of all ages are gathered. Some of the table groups appear to have two or three families working together on a project, some have teenagers or adults working together, and other table groups have people of all ages at them.

At the front or middle of the room is a large-group facilitator, or emcee, giving instructions to the groups and guiding them through the learning experience. Circulating throughout the room are catechetical leaders in brightly colored T-shirts assisting the table groups as needed, or who have been assigned to help facilitate the learning at one of the table groups.

Some of the younger children are participating in the learning experience with their families, while others have opted to attend the preschool learning option offered in another room.

The *whole group* format is a good choice for intergenerational learning when a parish has:

- a large physical space with good acoustics and sound system and appropriate furniture to comfortably accommodate the learners
- a competent large-group facilitator, capable of providing clear instructions and able to manage the dynamics and energy of a large group
- a group of catechists who feel comfortable moving through the assembly offering assistance, or a large-enough team of table leaders to assign one catechist to work with each table group
- a learning topic that lends itself to everyone learning the same thing at the same time but in different ways in the same space.

Timing in the *whole group* format is crucial. The various table groups must be able to accomplish the learning tasks in a similar time frame to prevent some table groups having to wait long periods for other groups to finish.

The *age group* format provides for three or more separate parallel learning groups to focus on the same topic through the use of learning activities best suited for their learning abilities.

Imagine the learning assembly has just completed their all-ages opening learning experience and participants are moving into various spaces in the parish facility. Families with preschool children have moved to the carpeted space of the school library for their learning time. Families with school-aged children have moved into one of the parish halls for their learning, and the teen and adult groups have also found a comfortable learning space. For the next hour or so all of the learning will take place in these parallel learning groups.

The *age group* format is a good choice for intergenerational learning when a parish has:

- an adequate number of meeting spaces in which the various groups can gather
- an adequate number of competent facilitators and catechists to work with each group
- a topic that is best explored through age-specific learning. Some topics are best explored using different activities for different groups.

The number of age groups may vary depending on your total number of participants. Here are some possible age groups:

- 3 years old and younger: child care
- 4 and 5 year olds (including kindergarten): pre-school program with one or more catechists in a separate meeting space
- parents with children in grades 1–5
- middle school/young adolescents in grades 6–8
- high school/adolescents in grades 9–12
- young adults (singles, married couples) from 18–39 years old
- adults who are 40+

You may decide to have fewer groups—such as putting all teens together, or putting young adults and adults together—if your overall numbers dictate such a choice.

The *learning activity center* format provides structured learning activities at a variety of stations or centers in a common area.

Imagine groups of learning teams, whether age-specific or intergenerational, busy at a variety of learning activity centers in the parish complex. After a twenty-five minute learning period, the parish complex erupts into temporary chaos as the learning groups move from one learning center to the next.

The *learning activity center* format is a good choice for intergenerational learning when a parish has:

- a large physical space where multiple learning centers can be set up without each center being too noisy or distracting for other centers, or a parish complex that has multiple meeting or classrooms in which the centers can be hosted
- an adequate number of catechists or facilitators to guide the learning at each center, or activities that are simple enough for learners to guide themselves
- a learning focus that lends itself to exploration through a variety of shorter topics that are facilitated through a variety of methods, such as a scripture drama and discussion, making something together like an Advent wreath, a video with a response activity, and so on.

Whole Group Sharing Experience This portion of the learning event helps participants share what they've learned with each other, and discover ways to apply the learning to their lives.

The whole group sharing experience provides an opportunity for each learning group to share some highlights of their in-depth learning experiences with the rest of the community. Groups may describe the project or activity they created, give a verbal summary, share a symbol of their learning, offer a dramatic presentation, and so on.

Whole group sharing can be conducted in small groups sharing their learning activities—for example, families with children, youth, young adults, adults—or conducted with presentations to the entire learning assembly.

Personal or Household Reflection After the whole group sharing, learners are invited to move to personal application of their learning. Through reflection, participants can integrate what they have learned into their lives. Only then will they experience change and growth.

In the "present," you will ask participants to reflect on their learning experience by responding to simple openended sentences such as "I learned… I discovered… I was surprised by… I was moved by…" After a period of reflection, they share with a partner or table group.

For the "future," you might give participants a postcard in their take-home resources (see home application below) with the same open-ended sentences. After participating in the event for which the learning session was preparing them, they fill out the card and drop it in the collection basket. These reflections may be shared anonymously with all parishioners through the parish bulletin or by other means.

Home Application Participants are given an opportunity to craft a concrete action plan for how they will live out what they have learned. It may be as simple as a to-do list or a pledge card. The learners are also given, with explanation and guidance as needed, any tools and resources they will need to continue the learning, praying, and serving at home. It is important that any skill (praying with or blessing another), be PRACTICED on site before the learners are sent home to implement it.

For example, home kits might include a table prayer for the season, reflections on the scripture readings, puzzles or activities, resources to add to a home altar, and so on.

Closing Prayer Service The closing prayer service reminds participants what the learning is all about: celebrating and building the Kingdom of God. Symbols and responses like pledge cards, prayers of intercession, action plans, and so on can be incorporated into a closing prayer service.

For additional explanation, information, and implementation tips for each of these components go to pp. 38-63 in the *People of Faith: Generations Learning Together Organizer's Manual* by Mariette Martineau, Harcourt Religion Publishers, 2005.

A Picture of the Dance

On an evening several weeks before the Feast of Pentecost, parishioners at Notre Dame began arriving at the parish center. As they entered the building, they were warmly welcomed and escorted to a table to await the evening meal. The table was decorated with red and white balloons, and there were various puzzles and activities about Pentecost on the table for the learners to use during the course of the evening. Once the seating space at the table was full, the learners recited the meal prayer from the stand-up card on the table and headed to the buffet to get supper.

As the meal wound down, the overview of the evening's session was presented and the learners got a sense of the evening's activities. The community-builder leader then distributed to everyone a small piece of paper with the picture of an animal on it and invited everyone to make the noises of that animal and to find all the other people with that animal on it to make a learning group. Once the learning groups settled into their designated tables, the story of the first Pentecost was shared, and the learners compared the noise of the animal activity to the noise and confusion of languages of the Pentecost experience.

The community was then called to prayer, a hymn of the Holy Spirit was sung, and a Pentecost sequence was prayed together.

The groups then did a Bible study together as the all-ages learning experience, reading the first Pentecost story from scripture and working through a multiple choice response form during which they imagined what it might have been like to have actually been at the first Pentecost experience.

One of the central catechists then stepped forward to begin the in-depth learning activity. She explained that their first task in their groups was to read a variety of scripture passages about the Holy Spirit and to create a symbol from craft foam to depict that image. The images were then attached to a wind sock for the learners to carry their images home with them. As the group completed their windsocks some noise and confusion was heard in the hallway and several clowns bearing a soup pot, a bag of supplies, and a large sign came dancing into the room. The clowns engaged the learners in exploring "Parish Minestrone Soup" as the learners made the connection between the salt the clowns had given them and the flavor of the soup. At the table groups the learners were then invited to consider the gifts (salt) of the Holy Spirit, their meaning, and how they themselves were called to share those gifts with the community. An age-appropriate gifts discernment tool was then given to all learners and they were invited to discern how they could share their gifts with their parish and local community.

Each learning group was then challenged to create a poster that summarized what they had learned about the Holy Spirit and Pentecost that evening, and were invited to share their poster with one other table group.

The Holy Spirit song that had begun the prayer service was sung again, and the learners were invited to briefly reflect on what they had learned that evening that they could take home and apply to daily life. Home kits were passed out and "walked through" so everyone knew what was in them (a table prayer for Pentecost, a scripture passage for each of the seven days before Pentecost, and a gifts-of-the-Spirit game). A simple prayer to the Holy Spirit was prayed together, and the learners were sent forth to transform the world. The learners didn't make a mad dash from the room, but rather hung about chatting and mixing with one another!

What Makes It Work?

Parishes practicing this approach to intergenerational faith formation cite many factors that help the dance to flow and be engaging for all learners. In the spring of 2007, the Center for Ministry Development invited parishes who had been implementing intergenerational learning through the *Generations of Faith* project to complete an online survey to share with us what they felt was most important about intergenerational learning. Two hundred seventy-six practitioners responded, and the following factors were identified as some of the "things a parish needs to do to ensure good intergenerational learning."

Variety Practitioners cited that variety was important: variety of opportunities for people to engage in, variety of learning options, variety of hands-on learning activities, a variety of blends of learning, sharing, and ritual, and overall providing creative activities. Key to the variety is that it serves to keep the learning interesting and informative. Parishes will change how they offer the in-depth learning experiences, so there is a variety of learning formats. Parishes will vary how they form groups, where they offer the learning (hall, worship space, and so on), and will vary who leads the learning so new faces and voices are heard. Amid all this variety, stability is also important. Learners should know that the general template of the learning, as described in the ten components above, will probably be the same, but look forward to variations of those ten components.

Timing Practitioners commented on how important timing is in the intergenerational learning dance. Because of the various attention spans of learners and the diversity of age groups in the room, it is critical that presentations are not too long and that activities are broken into manageable units so they do not take too long to explain. And it is important that large group facilitators pay attention to the ebb and flow of the energy in the room, making shifts to the program as needed. Sometimes the shift is to extend the time of the program element, for example sometimes the group is intensely engaged in table discussions and needs more time to finish those off, or sometimes a speaker has sparked a lot of questions in a group and needs time to adequately answer them.

Team leadership Again and again practitioners cited how vital team leadership is to the successful implementation of intergenerational learning. Practitioners cited that "dedicated volunteers with the same vision" is important as it makes the creation of the intergenerational session and its facilitation flow much easier. Leaders said that it is important to include all ages in the planning process to ensure that all learning needs are met, and that the "cooperation of catechists who have a willingness to change and learn" made planning and implementation more solid.

Bottom line, all those on the team must have a common vision and the willingness to work collaboratively and creatively together.

Open to the Spirit In the dance of intergenerational learning, as in all good learning, space for the Holy Spirit (time and relational presence usually) is needed. Parishes "must be open to what intergenerational learning can provide for a parish community." Good planning and organization lead to greater flexibility in implementation! Practitioners in the survey often cited how important it is to have "sessions that are well planned," "advanced preparation," and "easy-to-follow lesson plans."

Welcoming environment No one likes to learn in a space where they do not feel welcome. As one leader said, the intergenerational learning session needs to "be a welcoming environment for all ages to participate," and another said that it needs to be an "inviting flexible atmosphere for all ages." Have you ever noticed that in some parishes adult hospitality ministers will engage in conversations with the adults they are welcoming but seldom acknowledge or attempt conversation with teens or children? That's not the type of hospitality parishes are implementing at their intergenerational learning. Rather, they are inviting leaders of all ages who feel comfortable to welcome and interact with people of all ages.

Clarity of goals Parishes trained through the Center for Ministry Development are challenged to clearly cite their learning objectives for their intergenerational learning sessions:

- *Know what*: What theological learning about the event or content does the parish need?
- *Know how*: What do we want parishioners to be able to do better through participating in this learning?
- *Know why*: What do we want parishioners to better value through their participation in this learning?

Practitioners said that having a clear message enables both the planners to prepare and the learners to learn more effectively.

Passion and commitment No one likes to learn with catechists and facilitators who appear to be bored with their own content. Parishes said that it was important to "show enthusiasm when talking about the program," to have "interested leaders," and that the "enthusiasm of both presenters and attendees" has an impact on the learning that occurs.

Good facilitators Intergenerational learning may require a parish to "dig deeper" for facilitators, inviting and working with people who have different skills and comfort zones than traditional catechists. Parishes say that the "presenter needs to be respected and knowledgeable," "able to engage everyone," and have "theological background."

In the facilitation of the whole group format, a large group facilitator is needed who is able to work with large groups and keep the learning "dance" moving and focused.

Know the audience Some parishes find that drama works well with their group of learners, others find that their parish loves learning through game shows and interactive games. Practitioners say that it is important to "know your audience" and to "know the needs of your community."

The needs of your community will help you to ascertain what learning topics should be addressed and in what order. They will also help the team to incorporate current issues and topical opportunities into the learning sessions.

Need to engage all learners Intergenerational learning is not a passive learning experience. It simply is not possible to engage learners of all ages in a passive style of learning like ninety-minute lectures. The art of intergenerational learning is that no one is sitting on the sidelines observing while someone else learns. All are actively engaged in the learning.

In the words of practitioners, you need to have "involvement from all generations," "make it interesting for all ages," "use active learning techniques," create "good interactive lesson plans that offer growth experience for all," provide "age-appropriate resources," and use "material that excites or sparks interest."

Textbooks and handouts have been a large part of parish catechesis. In an intergenerational context, handouts are primarily used as guides or as worksheets, versus the means for which the content is delivered. For example, during the tour of the Mass, a handout with a "map" of the liturgy is given to participants. The adults will use it as a visual guide and the children will use it to physically draw small footprints to mark the learning journey.

Activities like crafts are not done simply for the sake of doing a craft, but are intimately linked to the catechetical content. For example, if an Advent wreath is being created, each part of the creation process will have catechetical information attributed to it. The circle is explained before it is created, the participants are invited to ponder signs of hope as they create the leaves for the circle, and so on. Nothing is done that does not have catechetical significance or meaning.

Active learning does not equate to providing complicated learning experiences, but if one respects the learning principles laid out in chapter three of this book, good learning will be had by all.

Meaningful learning experiences The reality is that people of all ages want to invest their time and energy in learning that is worth their investment. In today's world with so many options tugging at our time, people want good quality for their time. As one practitioner said, "provide quality, theologically sound, yet interesting sessions that are worth the time commitment required." The tension is to provide interesting content that is solid and well designed.

It is important for parishes to continually evaluate their inter-generational learning offerings to make sure that both their content and their process are meeting the needs of learners.

Good materials and resources Practitioners are quick to point out the need for "good resources that cover all generations and languages." Some of the best intergenerational learning resources can be found in the *People of Faith* series from Harcourt Religion, and from the Center for Ministry Development's subscription Web site, www.generationsoffaith.org.

For many, intergenerational learning is a new experience, so though there is some room for "learning by trial and error," it is important to note that a bad learning experience, often caused by not using good resources, can seriously affect attendance at future learning events.

Space Space for intergenerational learning is often a challenge, as many of our parish structures were built for the classroom model of learning. Parishes dream of "facilities conducive to the learning style" and have been incredibly creative with their use of space.

Prayer Prayer is not an "add on" to intergenerational learning but a central component. Practitioners said that "opening/closing prayers which involve the participants (symbolism, ritual, etc.)" are essential to the learning sessions. Music, strong proclamation of the word, a clear and visual presence of symbols and images through the art/décor and rituals, and capable presiders are important elements in the design and implementation of prayer.

Pastor support and presence Again and again, through the survey, leaders cited how important the role of the pastor is to intergenerational learning. The support of the pastor in both the promotion of the learning and in attendance at the learning session was mentioned by 25% of the survey respondents.

Pastors are involved in many ways. Some sit on the core team helping guide the "big picture decisions." Some like to contribute to the design or serve as the theological adviser to the design team, while others regularly serve as facilitators in the learning event itself. Some simply attend the learning sessions and lend support and encouragement to those in leadership and take advantage of the opportunity to build relationships with members of their parish.

Miscellaneous, yet important The following comments were only mentioned once in the survey responses but are worth mentioning here as they have been heard orally in many training groups:

- The intergenerational learning options need to be a "continuous program, not just a couple times a year."
- The all ages opening activity needs to be good to get the learner's attention.
- Be consistent.
- Research and study the topic thoroughly.
- Keep it simple.
- Be faithful to church teaching.

While just one parish mentioned that it is important to provide "an age-appropriate formation piece for each session," our ongoing consultation with parishes shows some experimentation in this regard. Some parishes offer a learning track for parents and elementary aged children, and see great benefit in a ten to fifteen minute adult oriented presentation to the parents while the children are engaged in music and drama related to the topic, followed by the two moving back into a learning group together. Sometimes teens and adults start out in separate learning groups then rejoin to have conversations about what they learned. In the home kit materials it is also important to remember to include some age-appropriate resources.

Conclusion

The dance of intergenerational learning can be a complicated and complex choreographed masterpiece, or it can be the simple choreography of a classical waltz. Whatever the complexity, parish leaders will tell you that by being intentional about the practices and elements addressed in this chapter, the dance will lead your parish community into great learning that will produce many fruits, as explored in the next chapter.

CHAPTER SIX

Evaluation of Learning

How does one measure something as nebulous as faith? How does one know if learning is taking place in the intergenerational learning context?

The traditional measure of whether learning is taking place for adults, especially in the corporate world, is related to skills, knowledge, and attitudes. Have the adults learned new skills? Do they have increased or deepened knowledge of the content area? Do they value something in a new or different way?

For children, the prime elements traditionally measured are cognitive comprehension and motor skills, whether in the arts, handwriting, or in the gym.

The definitive aim of catechesis as defined by the *General Directory for Catechesis* is "to put people not only in touch, but also in communion and intimacy with Jesus Christ" (#80). How does one measure that? Is it measured by how much of one's income is shared with the church and those in need? Is it measured by how many hours or days a person volunteers their gifts in service? Is it measured by how the world is now a better place because of a parish's faith formation offerings?

The goal for catechesis is transformation for discipleship; of the individual, community, and world, so that the light of Christ is brightly shining everywhere.

Most Catholic parishes in the US, and many who are implementing intergenerational catechesis, have not invested much time or energy in documenting or tracking the learning that has been taking place. Parishes are busy implementing, and are happy to see that learning is taking place. They have little time or means to measure the amount and impact of the learning. Yet, evaluation of learning is something that should be done, provided the right things are evaluated. As the NDC says, "Catechetical planning should include…periodic review and evaluation" (#58). If the goal is Christian discipleship, we need to be creative in how we ascertain whether our learners are living that out.

This chapter will explore how parishes implementing intergenerational learning most often evaluate the learning taking place. We will then show what the 276 practitioners who responded to the *Generations of Faith* survey in spring of 2007 said in response to these two questions: "What fruits have been produced by your implementation of lifelong event centered intergenerational learning?" and "If someone were to ask you, 'how do you know learning is taking place through the intergenerational learning sessions,' what would you say?"

What Are Parishes Doing?

One of the most common ways that parishes evaluate their intergenerational learning sessions is through evaluation forms distributed at the end of each learning session. As one practitioner said, "Our evaluations help us to explicitly know" if learning is taking place. The evaluation forms usually include the following:

- Reaction to the learning—did they like the learning experience
- Citing of one or two points that they learned in the session
- Questions that they have about the topic

Practitioners also employ the "interview" technique, taking time at the sessions, after the sessions, and in other venues, to have one-to-one conversations about the learning experience.

One practitioner noted that they "present self evaluations at various gatherings and more and more people are pleased that they do well, and we also are impressed with what they have learned. This is one tool that we have used with success." Another evaluation technique related to self evaluations is challenging participants to a pre-and-post test. Participants are given a true/false or multiple choice test before the learning session takes place to score their current knowledge. At the end of the learning session, they take the same test to see if their knowledge has increased.

Table facilitators and catechists are also consulted about their insights on whether learning is taking place. A simple debriefing process at the end of the intergenerational learning session enables leaders to share what happened with their groups, as well as enabling them to share what further questions the learners raised about the topic. Experienced facilitators know that one of the best ways to see if learning is taking place is through the content and type of questions raised by the learners. For example, do the questions indicate that the learners are probing more deeply into the content? Are the learners asking or suggesting how to apply the information in other contexts? Are the learners asking questions that lead to further clarity about the topic?

One practitioner said that she "uses face-to-face evaluation focus groups to identify successes and challenges." Focus groups are efficient ways to gather diverse groups of people for their feedback.

Other parishes use game show formats to test the group's learning. One parish plays a trivial pursuit game using information from the previous learning session as the content. Another practitioner cited that they "do a jeopardy review of every session." Evaluation of learning can be fun!

As mentioned in Chapter Five, part of the intergenerational learning format is the whole group sharing, during which participants give presentations about what they have learned. It is "through observing the small group presentations to the large group that recaps what they learned" is how one practitioner described how they evaluate the learning.

Some parishes involve "bring backs" to see what learning has taken place. Bring backs are activities that households do at home and then bring back. For example, a bring back might be an illuminaria bag decorated with symbols of Advent that they found in the scripture passages for Advent. Another parish challenged learners to count how many times the word baptism was mentioned in a take-home article and to cite the three central points about baptism that the article mentioned.

For the most part, these evaluation methods do not measure "practice" but cognitive comprehension of content. While not a bad thing, more work is needed to enable parishes to more deeply evaluate the learning that is taking place. The following section offers some insights about the various levels of evaluation needed.

Levels of Evaluation

A valuable resource that provides a window of understanding into evaluation and into the feedback that practitioners offered us about evaluation is the work of Donald Kirkpatrick. In 1959, Kirkpatrick developed a fourfold model for evaluating training and learning programs that is the most widely used approach to evaluating training in the corporate, government, and academic worlds. We believe it can also serve to help evaluate the learning that takes place in parish faith formation offerings, especially in the intergenerational realms.

The higher the level of evaluation, the more time, effort, and creativity are needed to assess the learning. Here is a description of the four levels.

LEVEL ONE: REACTION

As the word implies, evaluation at this level measures how participants react to the learning. This level is often measured with attitude questionnaires that are passed out after the learning experience. This level measures one thing: the participant's perception (reaction) of the course. Did they like it? Do they think they learned something from it? Do they have advice about how to make the learning better? Will they come back? The interest, attention, and motivation of the participants are critical to the success of any learning program. We know in parish life that it is hard to get people to return if they have a bad reaction to the learning that was offered.

LEVEL TWO: LEARNING

This is the extent to which participants change attitudes, improve knowledge, and increase skill as a result of attending the program. It addresses the questions: Did the participants learn anything? What knowledge was acquired? What skills were developed or enhanced? What attitudes were changed? Parishes that offer pre-and-post testing are trying to evaluate the knowledge of the learners. The challenge for catechists is how to evaluate practice. Does one evaluate how well one can pray? Or engage in stewardship? We often do not dare to evaluate attitudes or values, yet we write learning objectives that encompass all three of these components. Every learning session needs to include actual practice of the concepts taught, and this level of evaluation enables the participants and the facilitators to concretely evaluate whether or not learning has taken place.

Level Three: Transfer of Learning

In Kirkpatrick's original four-levels of evaluation, he names this level "behavior." Others sometimes refer to it as the transfer of learning. Can the learner take what they have learned in the intergenerational learning sessions and transfer it to their home, work, or school? This level of evaluation involves testing the participant's capabilities to perform learned skills "in the real world." Level-three evaluations can be performed formally (testing) or informally (observation). Obviously for us, when we consider why we do faith formation we want to SEE learners living out their faith—practicing prayer and ritual at home, using their Christian values to make decisions and live out their faith at work, sharing their gifts in service to others, and so on. This level of learning is still focused on the individual or household: are they able to transfer their learning, applying it in an integrated way in their lives? It is important yet very difficult to measure performance because it demands attention to evaluation outside of the learning setting. It also demands a mentoring system or a learning community in which participants are able to give concrete feedback to one another about how well they are transferring the learning.

Level Four: Results/Impact

This is the evaluation level that is the hardest to measure, yet it offers the most valuable information, for it raises the question, "what impact did the learning have on our entire community?" How is our community living differently because of the learning that we offer? Impact-level evaluation measures the program's overall effectiveness, that is, "What impact has the training achieved?" In a parish setting impact-level results would include such things as increased participation in liturgy, more people attending liturgical events, increase in volunteers and parish donations, increase in justice and outreach, and an overall sense that by deepening our relationship with Jesus Christ through catechesis we are brightening the broader community with the Good News. This impact might be discussed at the grocery store, "What are those Catholics doing these days? My neighbors have been attending some new learning sessions that they are offering and they've been more helpful than ever." Collecting, organizing, and analyzing level-four information can be difficult, time-consuming, and costly, but the results are often quite worthwhile when viewed in the full context of its value to the organization.

One tool that some parishes are currently using to measure at this level is Gallup's ME 25. Gallup's ME (ME stands for Member Engagement) assessment tool goes to the heart of an individual's and a congregation's engagement and spiritual commitment, giving congregations a clear picture of their spiritual health. Such a picture is crucial, for Gallup's research confirms that spiritual health drives all other factors—including attendance and financial commitment—in a congregation's life.

The ME tool consists of twenty-five items: nine items measure individual spiritual commitment, twelve measure congregational engagement, and four outcome items measure life satisfaction. The spiritual commitment items are individual and personal, while the congregational engagement items indicate how strongly one feels a sense of belonging within the congregation. Members who are highly engaged are more likely to give more money to their congregations and to volunteer more hours per week to help and serve others. They are also more likely to invite others to participate and to be more satisfied with the conditions of their lives. The same is true of members who are more spiritually committed. For more information, visit: http://www.gallupfaith.com/

As we move from Kirkpatrick's level one to level four, the evaluation process becomes more difficult and time consuming. However, it provides information that is of increasingly significant value. Perhaps the most frequently used type of measurement is level one (reaction) because it is the easiest to measure. However, it provides the least valuable data. Measuring results that affect the organization is considerably more difficult, thus it is conducted less frequently, yet it yields the most valuable information.

Reaction-Evaluation Feedback

As already mentioned, in the spring of 2007, the Center for Ministry Development invited parishes who had been implementing intergenerational learning through the *Generations of Faith* project to complete an online survey to share with us their insights about intergenerational learning. Thirty-two percent of the respondents said their parishes cited feedback (verbal and written) as their principal means to ascertain whether learning was liked or not (reaction-level feedback.) As one practitioner said, "at the end of each GOF session, we hand out questionnaires to get a feel for what was learned and was found to be interesting and/or new to the community."

Reaction-level feedback includes comments from learners and observers about participants' desire to come to the learning event. One practitioner said that "kids are excited about faith formation." Another said that "those who continue to attend GOF talk about it afterwards and at other functions." Someone else said that they feel affirmed that learning is taking place from "listening to the participants tell non-participants what happened."

The request from participants for more learning is another sign of positive reaction level feedback. As one practitioner said, "People began by asking questions and for additional info. They began to come to church, and to request specific topics, and attended sessions more frequently."

Watching the engagement of those attending the learning is another way to see if people are learning. A practitioner noted that "the engaging looks on the faces of the kids, the heartfelt sharing of adults" are signs for her that learning is taking place. As one practitioner said, I know learning is taking place by "watching how engaged the various age levels are, from young children to adults." Another said that "You can see the intensity on the faces of both the adults and the children as they learn together. In the large group sharing, the responses show learning is happening." One practitioner made the link to sacramental preparation, "It has been noted that during parent meetings/preparation sessions for sacramental programs, parents are much more interested than in the past. They look forward to prep sessions; they don't act bored."

Sometimes adults in particular are surprised by their own learning. As one practitioner said, "Some folks just tell me that they have learned so much from sessions that they thought were for their children."

Reaction-level feedback may also be observed through the numbers of those in attendance. If numbers go down or up for no apparent reason (if it's not due to softball or hockey starting, or scheduling conflicts) then organizers must figure out how to interpret the number change. Several practitioners cited on the survey that "return participation" and "the increasing number of people attending and volunteering at GOF sessions and liturgies" is a sign that learning is happening. This comment "We are a small parish (370 families on the books) and we always have over 200 people at each GOF session" is a good sign that the learning is well received. "They keep coming back and telling us they love it and that it helps them as a family to focus."

Overall, the sense from the thirty-two percent of the 276 practitioners whose feedback indicated reaction-level feedback is that the learning has been positive. "Families leave excited about what they've experienced and we get good evaluations."

Learner Evaluation Feedback

One of the groups that is mentioned again and again on the survey in relation to whether or not learning is taking place is adults. One of the reasons adults are probably mentioned so often is that in most parishes attracting adults to faith formation has been challenging, and many parishes in the past have chosen to invest the majority of their resources in children. We assume children are learning because we gather them, so it's exciting to see adults gathering for learning in more ways now too! Through intergenerational learning, parishes have been able to reach and teach more adults than they ever have before. As one survey respondent said, the intergenerational learning is "the most adult education ever in our parish—and quality too." When asked the open-ended question "How do you know learning is taking place through intergenerational learning?" twenty-four percent of respondents specifically referred to the adult participant saying that they either liked the experience or were learning. When asked the open-ended question, "What fruits have been produced by your implementation of lifelong event-centered intergenerational learning" eighteen percent of respondents mentioned that adults are learning about their faith.

One parish said that their regular adult attendees have told them "that they have learned more in GOF than they did in twelve years of Catholic school." This isn't a criticism of Catholic schools, but rather an affirmation of the adult faith formation. Numerous practitioners offered remarks similar to this one, saying that adults have "expressed that they have learned so much from the sessions. Our pastor conducts the adult sessions and offers a great deal of insight and background." Another practitioner said that "people express appreciation for what we are doing. We hear a lot of 'I never knew that' and 'It's been a long time since I've thought about that' and 'I never understood things this way before.'" One practitioner said that "the number-one comment from adults is, 'I never realized how much I'd forgotten.'"

Parishes are citing an increase in knowledge. "Parishioners are more knowledgeable about what the Catholic Church teaches."

Other practitioners cited that they believe learning is taking place by the requests for more learning. "Discussions continue beyond the learning session. There is a growing hunger for additional learning opportunities on these topics."

Learner-level evaluation can also be tracked by the retention levels of the content and concepts from the learning sessions. As one practitioner noted, "Learners are able to bring up concepts from prior festivals and years."

In the spring 2007 survey of practitioners several (six percent of respondents) noted that they are not sure if the learning is taking place. Only one respondent said, "I don't think it (learning) is taking place." Their responses were simple: "unsure," "unknown," "I wish I could say this (that learning is taking place) but I'm not sure," a simple "I don't know," and an honest admission that "we haven't done enough yet to judge this." Without concrete measurement no one knows for sure if learning is taking place, but ninety-four percent of the practitioners who responded to the survey believe that learning is happening.

Transfer/Behavior Level Feedback

As mentioned earlier, the higher one moves through the levels of evaluation, the harder the task of measuring the learning. How does one measure, beyond verbal or written feedback from the participants, if participants are carrying the learning to their homes, schools, and work places? Parish staffs rarely have enough time to design and facilitate the learning sessions, let alone follow the learners into their daily lives to see if they are transferring what they have learned. One practitioner said that they had done a survey, and from that survey they discovered "that families are praying at home and practicing faith at home, and have renewed enthusiasm about their faith."

In the survey responses, one can see that many practitioners believe that the transfer of learning is happening. Forty-one percent of survey respondents agreed with the statement, "Families are practicing their faith more regularly at home." One practitioner said that "parents know what their children are learning and can expand on the subject at home." Another said "Parents and children are connecting in ways they never did before and the parents tell me it is helping in their overall relationship with their children."

Practitioners are often most concerned about the transfer of learning to the home, and one practitioner confidently said, "I know families who are having dinner together and are having conversations at that dinner about faith. I know families whose youth are now attending youth group and are coming to Mass more regularly." One practitioner who is also a parent said, "My child asks me questions about what she discussed during her session, related to other activities that take place later on." Another talks about the feedback received from parents, "Parents have told me they are discussing things at home that they never would have without GOF presentations and home activities—I feel it's all about recognizing sacred moments in our everyday lives."

Practitioners find that learners approach them in other contexts: "Many people stop me after Mass and tell me what they are doing at home and how their families have grown throughout our learning sessions. Also their children can't wait to come to the next session."

Most of the practitioners who completed the spring 2007 survey are in parishes whose intergenerational offerings are event centered, that is, they prepare learners to participate in upcoming events (church year feasts and seasons, sacraments, and so on) in the parish. Because of the event-centered focus, part of the transfer of learning is connected to the ability to participate in the event. Forty-eight percent of respondents agreed with the statement: "Parishioners are better prepared to participate in parish events" and that this is a "fruit" of their intergenerational learning. One practitioner noted that "The assisting priests at the first reconciliation commented that this year's participants were the best prepared they've seen in years." Another noted that there was "greater participation in the Triduum." "Faith growth is noticeable and measurable through increased participation and eagerness." Practitioners cite that "they can see it in the participation of practitioners in a variety of events," and "faith growth is noticeable and measurable through increased participation and eagerness."

"When I hear people say, 'I didn't know that' or 'I learned a lot' or 'I am going to stations this week' because they feel more comfortable, I know they are learning."

Faith formation without transfer of learning is faith formation without arms, legs, bodies; for if we are unable to take what we've learned with us into our real lives what real change can happen? Overall, once again, practitioners seemed to believe that what they were doing through their intergenerational learning was indeed being carried home and into the world.

Impact-Level Feedback

Impact level, the highest of Kirkpatrick's four levels, is the hardest to measure as it requires both before and after assessments of community life, pre-and-post measurement of attitudes in the community, and so on.

The practitioners who completed the survey seem to intuitively believe that their parish communities have indeed experienced cultural and organizational differences as a result closely linked to the parish's investment in intergenerational learning. In fact, thirty-one percent of the replies to the open-ended question, "What fruits have been produced by your implementation of lifelong event-centered intergenerational learning?" were impact-level evaluation comments.

Several practitioners noted that the intergenerational learning has positively affected staff and leaders growth. "Catechists and staff are growing as we prepare," and learning is taking place because of the "spiritual growth of the team."

Community is another impact-level change cited by practitioners. One practitioner shared that "young adults and seniors have a place to share, learn, grow," and another said that "people with disabilities are coming to an event where they can feel God's love." One said that there is "improved community building," and another that there is a "growing sense of parish identity." Seventy-six percent of respondents agreed with the statement that one of the fruits of their implementation of intergenerational learning is "parishioners are building relationships with other parishioners."

"In clustered parishes, it has helped to build relationships between the parishes and improved respect and trust. Watching three or four generations learning together is a gift." Other practitioners said that "we are becoming a close knit family. It is so obvious." and the "mixing of the four generations builds community."

Connected to community is the feeling of life: "There seems to be new joy in our parish. New people are sticking around. People are getting excited about being Catholic."

Another sign of organizational impact is increased involvement, which was cited by several practitioners. "More parishioners are getting involved in other parish activities," the learning has been "empowering people to take on leadership roles in the parish," "some people volunteered who hadn't in the past," "gifts and talents of the parishioners are being revealed," "we see more families at Mass," and "more people are coming forward and requesting to get involved in something."

One practitioner cited that "Changes are being made in parish communication. Organizations are beginning to work together." That is serious impact!

Another practitioner cites that new initiatives have surfaced as a result of the learning, "Our year of focusing on social justice has led to a number of new initiatives for parish outreach."

Cultural change is impact-level feedback. Enabling a parish community to value learning as lifelong is a huge cultural shift away from the "graduation mentality." One practitioner said that "lifelong learning is becoming more the norm." Another specifically mentioned that "high school education continues after confirmation." One practitioner mentioned that we are "building a culture that supports lifelong learning." Reality is that parishes are making a shift to "focus on all instead of the kids only," as one practitioner said, and that is a major organizational change.

Catholics are not well known for their ability to evangelize others. Nurturing that attitude and value in a parish is another large impact change. One practitioner believes that their parish is doing that, "I have found that the intergenerational events we have held (now going on three years), have brought life and the Spirit into the lives of the people who attend and they are spreading the word!" Another practitioner affirmed that in this comment: "The people that attend are beginning to evangelize and bring more people with them to each session."

Judging by the number (thirty-one percent of responses) of impact-level comments made on the survey, practitioners do believe that through intergenerational learning they are having impact on the life and practice of their faith community. It is this awareness of the organizational impact that intergenerational learning will be seen, and is already seen by some, as a credible and critical track for parish faith formation. It is not a passing trend or something to be temporarily put up with, but is a central and Spirit-driven path to the renewal of faith formation that creates practicing disciples.

Conclusion

Granted, the data presented through Kirkpatrick's four levels of evaluation above as gathered through the spring 2007 online survey is "soft." Parishes are not engaging in elaborate plans for evaluation, and sometimes they fail to carry out even basic levels of evaluation. Should they be? Of course they should, but we all recognize the limitations of time, money, and expertise to do so. All the while, many are busy creating good contexts for learning to happen. And they believe and trust that they are offering their communities a great path to deepen and expand their call as disciples.

Our challenge to practitioners is to be more intentional about evaluation, so that through the tremendous work and energy being placed into intergenerational learning, church leaders will be able to be concretely shown that learning is happening. Participants in intergenerational learning, according to the practitioners surveyed, are liking the intergenerational faith formation context, and they are learning what the planners hoped they would. They are applying the concepts into their lives, and the world and parishes are better places because of it!

End Notes

Kirkpatrick, Donald L. *Evaluating Training Programs: The Four Levels.* San Francisco: Berrett-Koehler Publishers, 1994, 1996.

CHAPTER SEVEN

Times, Places, and Opportunities

Then afterward I will pour out my spirit upon all mankind.
Your sons and daughters shall prophecy, your old men shall
dream dreams, your young men shall see visions…. (Joel 3:1)

In order for the young to hear and learn from the dreams of their
elders, in order for the old to be comforted and inspired by the dreams of
youth, we need times when the generations can come together to share
their faith and learn from one another.

Intergenerational learning provides a rich context for faith formation,
as do age-specific and home settings. Effective catechesis takes place
when each of these three settings is used in harmony to meet the learning
needs of parishioners of all ages and at all stages on the faith journey. Just
as faith formation leaders seek to provide a variety of learning *methods*
to meet the diverse needs of parishioners, they also need to provide these
different settings.

Intergenerational learning has many benefits as a setting for faith
formation. It creates opportunities for further dialogue across generations
on the topics covered because all ages are exposed to the same faith
themes. Since we live in intergenerational contexts in our everyday
lives—at home, at work or school, at leisure—it is important that we

are comfortable sharing *faith* as readily as we share other aspects of life with people from different generations. Another advantage is sharing the gifts which each generation brings to the others: the wisdom and life experience of the elders; the questions and fresh insights of youth and young adults; the pure faith and innocence of the children. When age groups stay segregated throughout their faith formation, they never get the opportunity to be stretched by the journeys, experiences, and wisdom of the other generations.

Of the three settings mentioned above, the age-specific setting is the most established. Nearly every parish has age-specific faith formation programs, particularly for children and teens, and most have been running those programs for a long, long time. There are many opportunities for taking traditional age-specific programming and adding an intergenerational connection with the wider parish community and/or the home. This chapter will look at the various ways that intergenerational faith formation can be incorporated into a parish's systematic plan for lifelong catechesis.

Teaching the Core Curriculum

A valuable exercise for parish faith formation teams is identifying the basic curriculum for their parishioners: the core teachings of the faith that every person, young or old, needs to know. While it takes time to name the most important and most basic content the parish will cover in a given year, it is a fulfilling process. Once the core curriculum has been identified, the team must then determine which parts of the curriculum will be addressed in intergenerational settings, and which parts will be covered in age-specific, home-based settings, or included in sacramental preparation programs.

Ideally, the catechetical team would then seek to link the core curriculum to the *events* of parish life. The core teachings of our faith are imbedded in what we *do* as Catholics: Sunday worship, celebrating feasts and seasons, engaging in works of mercy and works of justice, building community among ourselves, and so on. What we are suggesting here is event-centered learning which prepares people to celebrate what we *do*, invites them to experience the event, and then helps them reflect on its meaning and apply it to their daily lives in appropriate ways for all ages learning together. This catechetical approach responds to the directive in the *General Directory for Catechesis*, which states: "It is from the whole life of the church that catechesis draws its legitimacy and energy" (GDC, #168). Since all ages are invited to participate in the events of church life, all ages learning the "know-what, know-how, and know-why" of these events makes sense.

The content to be covered will often determine which setting to emphasize. There are certain catechetical topics that need age-specific content and explanations, while other topics are enlivened by cross-generational sharing and reflection. For example, teaching about the sacraments lends itself naturally to intergenerational learning. Sacraments are meant to be celebrated in community, so learning about them in community makes sense. By contrast, moral issues are taught more readily in age-specific settings because the understanding of morality and moral decision making is developmentally dependent.

Age-Specific Learning

The *General Directory for Catechesis* reminds us that "It should not be overlooked that the recipient of catechesis is the whole Christian community and every person in it" (GDC, #168). For many parishes, the biggest challenge in implementing lifelong faith formation is recognizing and responding to the age groups in the "whole Christian community" who are currently left out.

One reality in parishes is the exit of many youth from religious education after eighth grade or confirmation, youth ministry, or Catholic high school graduation—whichever comes first. Another challenge is the lack of faith formation for young adults, middle adults, and seniors. Finding a good balance of age-specific and intergenerational learning experiences is one way to meet these challenges and support parishioners in continuing their learning throughout life.

MONTHLY FAITH FORMATION

Many parishes are modifying the weekly model of faith formation. They may maintain a weekly schedule, but utilize a different setting each week. For example, some parishes address the basics of their core curriculum through an intergenerational session for all ages one week, followed by two weeks of age-specific learning for children and adolescents, followed by one week of learning activities for families and households to do on their own.

Other parishes offer intergenerational sessions one week followed by three weeks of age-specific learning. Still others have adopted new approaches to the age-specific learning while maintaining monthly intergenerational sessions. They may offer the children's programs in six-week series in the fall and the spring. Some parishes are exploring week-long thematic learning experiences for their children which are modeled after a vacation Bible school format, teaching one theme in the summer for five days.

In each of these examples, the basics of the core curriculum is addressed in the monthly intergenerational sessions. The curriculum is complemented and extended via age-specific learning and home learning. The resources for the home learning are given out at the intergenerational session. The "home kit" includes simple rituals and prayers, short articles on the topic covered in the session, scripture connections, ways to live out the spirit of the teaching through service to the broader community, and family enrichment activities.

With any of these scenarios, sacramental preparation continues as before—with some nuances. Woven into the sacramental preparation program is the expectation that candidates (RCIA, First Eucharist, parents of babies to be baptized, engaged couples) will participate in the intergenerational faith formation sessions, for therein lies the core learning of the community. In the same way that we expect these candidates to worship on Sunday, we expect them to learn with the community in these sessions. Also, sacramental preparation leaders must adjust their specific curriculum according to the topics covered in the intergenerational sessions.

Saint Edith Stein Parish in Katy, Texas, takes an intergenerational approach to faith formation. Chris Twardowski, the director of faith formation, works with her team to choose a catechetical theme each year. In August, the parish has a kick-off to introduce the topic to the parish. A "luau" is held next to celebrate the launch of a new season of faith formation. Over the next nine months, nine intergenerational faith festivals are held (with each session being offered three different times). In one year their catechetical theme was "Creed," addressing the core topics of our profession of faith. The next year the parish chose the Liturgical Year as the catechetical theme. The intergenerational sessions are supported by vacation Bible school for the little children, RCIA and the Children's Catechumenate, sacramental preparation, which includes sponsors and candidates learning together, children's retreats and family retreats. All of these help fulfill the goal at Saint Edith's of "one generation passing on the faith to the next generation."

Janet Elwer leads the faith formation team at Sts. John & Paul Parish in Altoona, Iowa, in creating a systematic catechetical program. Their intergenerational faith formation, titled "Journey in Faith," also focuses on a key theme each year. The parish offers nine intergenerational sessions annually, with each session offered three different times. RCIA candidates are part of the Journey in Faith process, as are sacramental preparation families. Teens are encouraged to participate in Journey and are invited to take leadership and service roles in the monthly sessions. In addition to the sessions, Sts. John and Paul offers an intergenerational vacation Bible school and family-centered sacramental preparation. For First Eucharist, parents and children come to learning sessions together, where they experience both intergenerational learning centers and separate, age-appropriate learning. The parish has preschool catechesis, Theology on Tap for young adults, Christian Experience Weekends, small Christian communities, men's and women's Bible Study, Tables for Two, Life and Faith Connection, and Children's Liturgy of the Word. The parish also has an up-to-date library and website with links to many good web resources for independent learning.

These illustrations are examples of parishes using a variety of settings and formats to create a systematic approach to catechesis, not just for children, but for all ages. The content is laid out and then slotted into the monthly intergenerational sessions. The topics not covered are intentionally included in other settings: adolescent catechesis, small-group experiences, sacramental preparation, etc. These parishes have created a rhythm for busy parishioners to help them know what to expect, when to expect it, and how to work their schedules around the parish's faith formation.

Since many parishes have chosen textbooks with a spiral curriculum for their children's catechesis, it is easy to match a thematic chapter from the textbook with the theme being covered in the intergenerational session.

Once catechists get beyond the stress of teaching the themes in a different order from the Table of Contents, they begin to see how the textbook material and the intergenerational content can work in harmony to create a comprehensive curriculum.

Children in Catholic schools and their families can be connected to the intergenerational sessions, but it requires genuine collaboration between the faith formation team and the religion teachers in the schools. Teachers are asked to focus on the theme of the intergenerational session in the week leading up to the session, then to reflect with their students after the session. These teachers are in a good position to influence the extended learning at home by sending resources home on a regular basis, encouraging families to discuss what is being learned in the classroom along with what is being learned in the parish.

SEASONAL FAITH FORMATION

Some parishes have adopted a seasonal approach to the intergenerational portion of their faith formation. They select particular events of church life, such as Advent, Lent, and the Triduum, which occur every year and affect the lives of all ages in the community. Then they design intergenerational sessions to prepare the community to engage in each event by providing them with the "know-what, know-how, and know-why" of the event.

Tammy Norcross, the Director of Faith Formation at Sacred Heart Parish in Newton, Iowa, has found a unique way to blend several settings for catechesis to create a comprehensive parish program. During the year the parish has six intergenerational faith festivals, which are event-centered, and twelve weeks of small-group sessions, six in the fall and six during Lent.

Tammy offers the small-group sessions for all ages, but each group is essentially age-specific. The K-6 children use a lectionary-based curriculum for the 12 weeks. To include adults was a bit more challenging. One year Tammy offered lectionary-based small groups for adults but didn't have a great response. The following year she offered small groups on specific topics of social justice, so the adult small-group sessions became more focused. In 2006 the parish adopted *Why Catholic?* for the adult small groups. The number of adult participants in small groups grew to 120.

Tammy and her team now choose an annual faith theme, which is covered through all aspects of faith formation during that year. The six intergenerational faith festivals, done in the *Generations of Faith* format, and the small-group sessions cover the same theme. In 2007, the theme was liturgy and sacraments for GOF, complemented by the theme of sacraments for the adult small groups. Content covered in the intergenerational faith festivals is omitted from the sacramental preparation and the small-group series because the age groups will already have experienced that content at the festivals.

Once the yearly theme is chosen, Tammy puts the two six-week sessions for small groups on the calendar. Because Sacred Heart takes an event-centered approach to its intergenerational sessions, the team then chooses the six events of church life toward which they will prepare the community during those six sessions. The calendar for faith festivals looks different each year, but there is always a faith festival during the Advent and Lent seasons.

The faith formation leaders present the theme to the parish as the overall theme for the year and ask people to participate in all aspects of faith formation: GOF faith festivals, small-group sessions, take-home activities, and the church year events. Faith formation is seen not as separate activities from which parishioners pick and choose, but as one integrated program in which people are expected to participate.

Many parishes have chosen to offer intergenerational sessions during particular liturgical seasons like Advent and Lent. They continue with their age-specific religious education, but encourage families with children in faith formation programs to come to the all-ages experience by omitting class the week that the intergenerational session takes place. These parishes doing seasonal all-ages learning create a home packet as part of the experience so families and households can continue their learning at home.

OCCASIONAL FAITH FORMATION

A third version of mixing intergenerational learning with age-group learning involves choosing unique parish events which lend themselves to all ages coming together. Parish feast days, the dedication of a new church, or a new feature within the church or the parish, the pastor's anniversary or the parish anniversary, and Stewardship Sunday are examples. The parish designs the intergenerational sessions in preparation for these events while maintaining regular religious education classes.

Saint Clare of Assisi Parish in Houston, Texas, believes in family-centered and intergenerational learning experiences. Christy Wright, the Director of Intergenerational Faith Formation, described the structure of the parish's faith formation as being rooted in a commitment to family faith formation. Saint Clare's has ten intergenerational sessions each year. Four of them are full-parish *Generations of Faith* sessions. Recently they added a fall kick-off of faith, fun, and community building. One year the faith formation team also planned intergenerational sessions for All Saints, Advent, and the lenten mission, which culminated in a parish reconciliation service. The four sessions the following year included the fall kick-off, All Saints, Lent, and a Marian celebration in May.

The other six intergenerational sessions are part of Saint Clare's family faith formation. Families meet every other month and have the option of a Sunday morning or Sunday evening session. Parents meet with parents, enriching one another. Children are taught by catechists. Six times a year an intergenerational session replaces the regular process, and the generations learn together. There are also family service days in Advent and Lent and an annual family retreat.

Saint Clare's offers children's catechesis each week. The weekly classes include a home page for parents so the learning can continue at home, five parent newsletters a year, and a "Parent Guide to Prayer." Sacramental preparation, which the parish website describes as family-centered, includes a parent-child retreat, the "Jesus Day," before First Eucharist. Packets of materials are given to the parents and include both prayers and the sacramental theology that they need to prepare their child for the sacrament. Vacation Bible school happens annually. Adults are enriched in their faith through scripture study and Men's and Women's Spiritual Growth groups.

CONTENT DRIVES THE METHOD

Another way to make good choices about when to use the intergenerational setting for learning is to consider which topics are relevant to all ages and lend themselves to vibrant discussions among the generations. Take, for example, the topic of discernment and vocation. All of us are called by baptism to live faithfully in the world. We share the call to holiness, community, and service. At the same time, each one of us is uniquely called to a particular lifestyle—priesthood, religious life, marriage or single life—in which to live out our vocation. And we are challenged to discern to which vocation God calls us.

Parishes can explore the meaning of vocation in an intergenerational setting by doing the following:

- Conduct an opening prayer which celebrates all of the vocations.
- Keep all ages together for introductory learning on vocations and discernment.
- Move into age groups to explore what vocation means for each particular stage of life.
  - » *Families with children* can explore the meaning of the call to marriage and family.
  - » *Seniors* can reflect back on their vocation and look ahead to living out their call in retirement.
  - » *Young adults*, who are at the age when most people discern their life vocation, can listen to people from older generations share their passion for sacramental love in marriage, or for vowed religious life, or for the sacrament of priesthood or the diaconate, or for the call to live as a dedicated single.
  - » *Adolescents* can focus on the art of discernment, learning how to listen for God's call as they move toward young adulthood and career choices.
- Bring the generations back together to discuss what they have learned about discernment and vocation, enriching one another's understanding of the topic.
- Send them home with resources to aid their discernment process and to further unpack the meaning of vocation in their everyday lives.

Obviously, there are many ways to live out the church's description of doing catechesis: "Catechesis is nothing other than the process of transmitting the Gospel, as the Christian community has received it, understands it, celebrates it, lives it, and communicates it in many ways" (GDC, #105). Some parishes utilize monthly intergenerational sessions; others create a seasonal curriculum; still others do occasional intergenerational sessions. Fashioning a curriculum that uses any of these forms of intergenerational learning in partnership with age-specific learning makes the church's vision a reality.

Creating Alignment

One way to make the parish's catechesis more intergenerational is to align the age-specific content with the other catechetical endeavors within the parish. In other words, intentionally fashion your catechetical curriculum so that all the age groups are being taught the same theme at the same time. The goal is to create opportunities for families, small faith-sharing groups, Bible study groups, parish ministries, and even committees to learn and discuss the same teachings at the same time.

Consider what alignment might look life for a family of five. The third grader and the sixth grader in their religious education classes and the sophomore in her youth ministry are all focusing on the Paschal Mystery of Jesus in age-appropriate ways. At the same time, Mom's parish pastoral council meeting begins with a prayer about Jesus' suffering, death, and resurrection, and Dad's Bible group is studying the passion as recounted by the four evangelists. This structure in itself is an invitation for further sharing at home about the meaning of the Paschal Mystery in everyday life. The whole family has a common theme to discuss over the dinner table.

In addition, if the parish sends home material for further discussion, families can extend the learning they receive at the parish. The home resource might be a short handout with three reflection questions for households to ponder together, or a simple ritual on suffering, dying, and rising in daily life for families to do together. It might be scripture passages with questions that help families break open the Word on the meaning of Jesus' suffering and death or a series of suggestions for how families can serve those who suffer the most in the world.

Publishers of Catholic textbooks who have intentionally chosen to use a spiral curriculum approach make it easy for parishes to create alignment, since the basic themes of Revelation, Trinity, Jesus Christ, Church, Morality, Sacraments, Kingdom of God, Prayer, Justice and

Service, and Church History are covered every year, in ever-deepening and age-appropriate ways. Collaboration among classroom teachers, youth ministers, sacramental preparation leaders, RCIA, and those responsible for adult faith formation can lead to all age groups learning the same theme at the same time.

A pastor in Omaha spent a year creating alignment among all of the ministries and the religious education in his parish. He and his faith formation team met to choose the "umbrella" theme for the upcoming year, which was discerned to be "sacraments." They then challenged every group meeting in the parish to align itself toward uncovering the meaning and purpose in each of the seven sacraments. Homilies connected the gospel message to being sacramental people at work, at school, at home, and in the world. The Bible study groups were asked to reflect on the scripture passages that birthed the sacraments. They studied their baptismal call, the gifts of the Holy Spirit, being a Eucharistic people, reconciliation with God and their neighbor, etc. *Catholic Updates* on the sacraments were placed in the church's reading rack, and parishioners were encouraged to take them home for reflection, study, and conversation.

When a particular age group celebrated a sacrament for the first time, the entire parish was invited to come together to deepen their understanding of the sacrament and to support those who were receiving Eucharist, the sacrament of penance, or confirmation. When the monthly baptisms of newborns took place, brief articles on the meaning of baptism and the role of the faith community in raising the newly baptized were published in the bulletin. When couples were married in the parish, "sound-bytes" from the actual rite of matrimony were sent to all married couples in the parish to review and renew their own lived experience of the sacrament.

As a result of the alignment, people of all ages began talking to one another about the sacraments and their meaning. People who had been married for forty-five years connected with the newly married. Instead of avoiding the Sunday Mass when babies would be baptized, out of fear that the Mass would take too long, people intentionally came to that liturgy to show support for the newly baptized babies and their families. Families at home felt connected to the parish, to the sacraments, and to each other's experience of the sacraments in new ways. In other words, the parish had made participation in the sacraments richer because people understood their role—as recipients of the sacrament or supporters of the recipient—better. And, to the delight of the faith formation team, conversations about faith became both accessible and natural.

Sacramental Preparation

One of the strengths of sacramental preparation programs in the last decade is the increased emphasis on involving parents and families in the preparation along with the candidates. This makes sense for several reasons. First of all, we live out our sacramental lives in the world, particularly in family life. The grace of each sacrament extends beyond the recipient of the sacrament to all whose lives are touched by that person. In addition, those receiving a sacrament benefit from the support of the faith community as they attempt to apply the effects and invitation of the sacrament in their daily lives. When parents and siblings are included in the preparation, the wisdom and experience of the parents can enrich the learning of the children. The pure innocence and trust of the children can re-inspire the parents to be faithful to the spirit of each sacrament.

Immaculate Conception Parish in Malden/Medford, Massachusetts, uses the *Generations of Faith* model of faith formation. The parish posts on its website a description of how parents are connected to the sacraments:

> Parents are an integral part of the preparation of the child to celebrate the sacraments of penance and Eucharist. There are preparation meetings for parents at which time they receive an update on the theology of the sacrament, as well as the "how to" prepare their child. We have an expectation that all parents of all our children will be an integral part of their faith formation. What happens at the parish should be a strengthening of what is already being practiced at home, such as daily prayer, weekly worship on Sunday, opportunities to teach Catholic Christian values through real-life experiences. Take some time during the week to review weekly readings with your child(ren). We are here to assist *you*, the primary teachers of the faith to your child(ren). (Shea and Connelly, www.icmalden.com)

On a practical level, including the siblings of the person receiving a sacrament, along with the parents, also makes sense. Before receiving the sacrament of penance, who is the recipient most likely to have conflict with if not family members? To whom does a second grader need to be the Body of Christ after receiving communion, if not to his or her brothers and sisters?

Expanding this concept, more and more parishes are including the godparents and grandparents in baptismal preparation. There are good print resources available for godparents, which explain their role as godparents. But it is also beneficial to bring the godparents into the preparation so that they can experience the theology of the sacrament as well as the implications for their unique role.

As a sacramental people, involving the whole community in learning more about a sacrament makes sense. Think, for example, about preparation for the sacrament of penance. In most parishes, children receive this sacrament in second, third, or fourth grade. They learn about the sacrament in their grade-level religious education program or their Catholic school. At the same time, many of these same parishes also hold a parish-wide reconciliation service sometime in the seasons of Lent and Advent. Why not link the two?

What if your parish decided to hold an intergenerational learning session on the sacrament of penance in late November or early December, or in late January or early February? All ages, including those who are going to receive their first reconciliation, come together to learn or re-learn the themes in this sacrament: conversion, penance, forgiveness, and reconciliation (CCC #1423-1424). The children are given the opportunity to share what they have learned in their class with the other generations gathered. When the parish holds its reconciliation service, the children make their first confession in the context of all ages participating in the sacrament. Later, generations come back together to share what the experience meant for them. The children again get the chance to share the meaning of their first reconciliation with the other generations in the parish.

A great opportunity for intergenerational learning happens when parishes look at ways to connect the catechumens in RCIA with those in the Children's Catechumenate. Saint Edith Stein Parish in Katy, Texas, aligns the calendars of the two groups so that they come together after their age-appropriate learning and dialogue on the aspects of Catholic identity they are discovering. They also share a retreat, with opportunities for meeting separately and together over the course of the retreat.

All of the sacraments are part of our Catholic identity. Exploring ways to connect all the generations to each sacrament enriches the life of the parish community as well as each individual who participates.

Expanding Adolescent Catechesis

One age group often segregated from the adults and children in faith formation settings is adolescents. Many parishes have no catechetical program for youth post-confirmation. Other parishes include catechesis as one of the components of youth ministry. As the U.S. bishops write in *Renewing the Vision*:

> Catechesis with adolescents recognizes that faith growth is lifelong and therefore provides developmentally appropriate content and processes around key themes of the Catholic faith that are responsive to the age-appropriate needs, interests, and concerns of young and older adolescents. (p. 29)

Renewing the Vision makes a case for the unique catechetical needs of youth, but also advocates for parental involvement as well as intergenerational settings:

> Catechesis with adolescents promotes family faith development through parish and school programs by providing parent education programs and resources, by incorporating a family perspective in catechetical programming, and by providing parent-adolescent and intergenerational catechetical programming. (p. 30)

Amy Auzenne, the director of youth ministry for St. Edith Stein Parish, models the parish youth ministry after the vision of RTV. The youth participate in the nine intergenerational learning sessions the parish does each year. In addition, Amy involves the youth in more age-specific catechesis—using the same theme the whole parish is studying in the nine sessions. Youth leaders serve on committees, with each committee being responsible for a youth night (held monthly). The committee takes an element of the parish catechetical theme and invites a young person to do a peer presentation on the chosen topic. One year the parish chose Creed as the umbrella theme. One of the topics the youth studied was "Do You Speak Catholic?" with the goal of helping young people understand the various phrases and expressions that are part of our Catholic Tradition.

Amy also makes intergenerational connections for the youth in the confirmation preparation program. Each young person is asked to commit to one year of parish ministry as part of the journey to confirmation. Many youth choose a ministry in which they are mentored by older parishioners, learning the "know-what" and "know-how" of the ministry from those mentors.

An important way to make an intergenerational connection in adolescent catechesis is to involve parents of teens. The youth minister at Immaculate Conception Parish in Malden, Massachusetts posts a note to parents on the youth ministry portion of the parish website. It includes the following suggestions under the banner of "How You Can Help":

> Remember that youth ministry begins at home! Immaculate Conception Youth Ministry can only supplement the Catholic Christian nurture you provide as a parent. Your Godly attention to and nurture of your son or daughter far outweighs what we can provide in a few hours each week. Model the importance of Jesus in your life. Adults need God as much as teens, and it's difficult to expect your teen to be more involved in Christian living and parish life than you. Pray for our ministry. Think and pray about getting involved. Opportunities for involvement range from a few hours occasionally to team teaching a session or leading a small group. We provide training and support for the job God calls you to do. (Morin, www.icmalden.com/parents.html)

Another way to make an intergenerational connection in youth catechesis is through service-learning experiences. When youth participate in service learning, the program usually focuses on providing adolescents with a good service experience while teaching them the church's rich social doctrines, especially the seven principles of Catholic social teaching. Parishes have sometimes involved the whole community in supporting the youth through prayer and fundraising. But a marvelous opportunity for intergenerational learning can happen when parishioners are invited to do more than these two things, important as they are.

Since the teens are learning about Catholic social teaching as they serve others, they are exposed to an area of Catholic identity that is not known to many older Catholics. Having the teens lead a parish intergenerational session on the meaning of the preferential option for the poor and vulnerable or the concept of solidarity when they return home from their service trip, empowers them to integrate what they learned while exposing the rest of the community to these Catholic social teachings.

Involving young adults and adults as chaperones on the service-learning trips can also lead to rich intergenerational dialogue on social teachings through the lens of different life stages and experiences. Programs like Young Neighbors in Action, which requires a teen/chaperone ratio of 5/1, provide a wonderful opportunity for adults from 21 to 71 to participate and learn along with the youth. Sometimes the deepest conversions on teen service trips occur in the hearts of the adult chaperones!

Vacation Bible School

Over the past several years, Catholics have awakened to the power of vacation Bible school to connect little children with God's Word. The results have been delightful, with young people singing scripture songs, creating crafts, and learning more about their faith through a week-long summer experience. Some parishes have taken this another step by involving parents in the VBS. Children share what they have learned through a presentation to their parents at the end of the week, and parents are invited to lead activities during the week. Sometimes take-home activities are provided at VBS so families can extend their learning at home.

Parishes that invite middle school and high school students to help with VBS have found that the adolescents benefit from the experience in several different ways. In addition to providing a real service to the parish, the teens discover the joys of scripture and learn about God's Word by teaching it to little ones.

More intergenerational connections can be made by inviting adult, young adult, and adolescent Bible study groups to reflect on the same passages from scripture that the children are learning in VBS, and then bringing all the Bible groups together to share with one another what they learned from God's Word. Another connection is made when the elderly, sometimes shut-ins, are invited to read and reflect on the same passages in a one-on-one partnership with a child participating in VBS.

Parishes that are doing intergenerational faith formation around the core curriculum are exploring ways of expanding the VBS format to teach older children as well as the little ones. Teens have also been invited into week-long focused catechetical experiences to cover the themes of faith identified by the bishops in *Renewing the Vision*.

Parish Mission

Many faith-formation leaders make their parish missions a top priority, often bringing in nationally prominent speakers to inspire parishioners with a fresh perspective on their faith. As great as many mission speakers are, they often direct their talks to the adults present (who usually compose the majority of the those who attend). When teens and children show up, they often tune out when the speaker doesn't seem to be connecting to their life experiences.

One way to engage different age groups in the mission is to ask the speaker to involve the parishioners in small-group discussion after each major point in the presentation. Depending on the content, these small groups might be age-specific or intergenerational. Because young people are familiar with interactive learning, the more they are engaged in the process, the more likely they are to be drawn in and inspired.

Another way to make the mission intergenerational comes from St. Edith Stein Parish. Chris Twardowski describes how the team developed their parish mission:

> While the adults were gathering with the speaker we brought in to do our mission, the youth had their own mission happening, complete with their own speaker and praise and worship, as did the elementary children, and very young children—and the nursery was full also! We aligned the missions for the youth and children with the topic of the mission for the adults. It was GREAT!

After the age-specific segment of the mission, all the ages came back together for a social. Chris had set them up for rich conversations. She also set up the households and families for discussion at home about the theme of the mission. Households, small faith-sharing groups, and friends were empowered to enrich their experience of the topic by seeing it from the perspective of others.

Asking guest speakers to provide questions and activities for parishioners to take home and do together can also extend the mission and create opportunities for families to engage in learning more about the topic together.

Conclusion

Good catechesis happens in many different settings and formats. There will always be a need for age-specific catechesis because of sacramental, developmental, and life-experience differences. There will always be a need for home-based learning because the family *is* the domestic church and the first place where people learn their faith. But the more we also offer intergenerational experiences to our faith communities, the more fruitful all of our catechetical efforts will be. Through a combination of all three settings—home, age-specific, and intergenerational—parishes fulfill the description of effective catechesis in the *General Directory for Catechesis*:

> Catechetical pedagogy will be effective to the extent that the Christian community becomes a point of concrete reference for the faith journey of individuals. This happens when the community is proposed as a source, locus, and means of catechesis. Concretely, the community becomes a visible place of faith-witness. It provides for the formation of its members. It receives them as the family of God. It constitutes itself as the living and permanent environment for growth in the faith. (#158)

Ultimately, the vision of the church—lifelong conversion and faith formation for each of its members—is accomplished uniquely in every parish community. Knowing all of the possibilities for creating a systematic, comprehensive, and intentional catechetical program in the parish sets up faith-formation leaders for success.

End Notes

Congregation for the Clergy. *General Directory for Catechesis.* Washington, DC: United States Conference of Catholic Bishops, 1998.

Libreria Editrice Vaticana. *Catechism of the Catholic Church: First Edition.* Washington, DC: United States Catholic Conference, 1994.

Shea, Sr. Margo, CSJ, Director of Faith Formation and Mrs. Elaine Connelly, Assistant Director. "Parental Involvement," Immaculate Conception Parish, a *Generations of Faith* Community. Malden/Medford, Massachusetts: Immaculate Conception Parish, as accessed on this web address on August 13, 2007: www.icmalden.com.

United States Conference of Catholic Bishops. *Renewing the Vision.* Washington, DC: USCCB, 1997.

Morin, Scott, Youth Minister. "How You Can Help," Immaculate Conception Parish, a *Generations of Faith* Community. Malden/Medford, Massachusetts: Immaculate Conception Parish, as accessed on this web address on August 13, 2007: www.icmalden.com/parents.html.

CHAPTER EIGHT

A Celebration of Best Practices

We know of many parishes that are in their fifth and sixth year of implementing intergenerational learning. As one practitioner recently noted, "I can't believe we're in year FIVE already! Doesn't seem possible—and yet, it seems like we've been doing this forever." Parishes like this have invested in a vision of faith formation that holds within it great contributions for the renewal of faith formation in North America.

At this late point in the book, you may still be wondering, "Can we do this?" or "Is it worth it?" Here we offer some of the best practices taking place in intergenerational faith formation, practices that will challenge you to imagine new possibilities and to be excited about what intergenerational learning might offer your community.

These practices emerge from the experiences of real parishes implementing intergenerational faith formation as part of their community's systematic catechesis. We interviewed leaders from several parishes engaged in these best practices of intergenerational learning. These leaders are merely representative of many others who are working just as creatively and effectively. In this chapter you will read about some of the best practices and experiences in the following parishes: St. Elizabeth of Hungary in Acton, Massachusetts; St. John the Baptist Parish in Mankato, Minnesota, St. Francis of Assisi Parish in Portland,

Oregon; Holy Trinity Parish of Webster County, Iowa; St. Michael and
Our Lady of Guadalupe Parishes in Cuero, Texas; Holy Cross Parish in
East Bernard, Texas; St. Mary Parish in Waverly, Iowa; St. John Brebeuf
Parish in Winnipeg, Manitoba; Holy Cross Parish in Euclid, Ohio; and
Resurrection Parish in Rochester, Minnesota.

Leadership for Intergenerational Learning

Parishes that engage in intergenerational faith formation know that it takes
more leaders to do this form of catechesis than is required to do classroom-
style catechesis. The traditional classroom model of teaching religion
typically involves adults who are trained as catechists for one particular
age group. With intergenerational learning, a variety of skills is required.
Many parishioners are tapped for potential leadership; consequently,
more people get involved in implementing the intergenerational learning
session.

It is sometimes challenging to recruit leaders for intergenerational faith
formation when it is new to the parish. Barbara Dane, the Director of Faith
Formation and coordinator of Generations of Faith at St. Elizabeth of
Hungary Parish in Acton, Massachusetts, said that at first Generations of
Faith was a foreign concept to parishioners, and so people were reluctant
to volunteer—they didn't know what it was they were volunteering to do.
But as the program has become more familiar to people, "every year there
is more and more willingness to assume leadership roles."

Mary Beth Nygaard, Director of Faith Formation at St. John the Baptist
Parish in Mankato, Minnesota, had a different experience. When the
parish first decided to explore intergenerational faith formation, eighteen
people signed up for the first training. As Mary Beth said, "That was a
real Holy Spirit moment for us." Having so many people come forward
was a clear sign that the parish was ready for intergenerational faith
formation.

The involvement of the pastor is crucial to the success of
intergenerational faith formation, but the type of involvement varies
according to the gifts of the individual. Some are master catechists and
enjoy teaching the entire community. Father Richard Colletti, the pastor
at St. John the Baptist and a very learned man, said he never learns
so much as when he prepares for an intergenerational session. Other

parishes have found their pastor taking supportive roles. In either case, a pastor's endorsement is key to success.

Including people from different ages on the core team and the design team is a hallmark of effective intergenerational planning. The core team sets the vision for faith formation in the parish, creates the curriculum, and manages the big picture in implementation. The design team is responsible for actually creating each intergenerational learning experience. In addition to the traditional invitation to adults to be leaders, teens and young adults are also needed to ensure that their learning styles, their questions and issues, and their faith needs are addressed in the learning sessions. St. John the Baptist Parish makes personal invitations to young adults to serve on the leadership and decision-making teams. The parish invites older teens to be catechists for the younger children. Caleb, a senior in high school, was quoted as saying he learned more from teaching the children than he did from attending the adult sessions.

Parents of children are needed to design activities that families can do together as they learn more about their faith with and from one another. And people with a background in theology are vital to the core team, since they bring the theological basis for the content being taught. Barbara Dane commented that St. Elizabeth invites parishioners doing graduate studies in theology at nearby Boston College to join the team. St. Elizabeth also rotates two or three core members in and out each year to get fresh ideas and to involve new leaders on a regular basis.

Effective intergenerational learning sessions rely on a gifted emcee to facilitate all of the movements within the session. This person is not necessarily an adult. Young people can hold the attention of a crowd just as well, if not better, than their elders. At St. Elizabeth of Hungary Parish, two of the best emcees are eleven years old. Barbara Dane describes these young leaders: "They're great. They're charismatic, and we love them!"

Since drama is a learning method that spans all ages, parishes have found creative ways to introduce the learning topic for an intergenerational session through the use of a lead character and a dramatic presentation. St. Francis of Assisi Parish in Portland, Oregon, has frequent visits from "Frank" (aka St. Francis), who helps parishioners enter into the learning experience. Thus, people with a gift for acting are brought into leadership roles.

There is a need for dynamic catechists in intergenerational learning. Sometimes a master catechist—someone uniquely skilled at engaging all ages in learning together—is required. At other times catechists for table groups are needed. These may be people who are good with adults, with youth, or with families with children. They may also be people who can guide a mixed-generational table group through the learning process.

Having people of different ages—including young people—who are trained as table leaders is also a plus. Teens can lead the youth tables, but are also capable of guiding a table group of mixed generations through a learning process which is being directed by the master catechist from the front of the room.

Another way people can get involved in leadership is by acting as guides for participants who move through learning activity centers. Parishioners who may not feel comfortable lecturing on a topic of Catholic identity may have the talent for leading a small group through a hands-on process which teaches the same content that the lecture would.

Other leadership roles at intergenerational sessions include planning and implementing the meal, the hospitality (providing a warm welcome, celebrating birthdays and anniversaries during the meal, doing a simple community-builder), and presiding over the prayer services. Barbara Dane shared that at St. Elizabeth they rotate people in and out of these roles so that more parishioners get the opportunity for leadership. With these particular tasks, there is less need to attend planning meetings, thus creating more willingness among busy people to say "yes" to a one-time commitment. Some parishes have established a guideline that people can take a particular role in intergenerational sessions once; if they volunteer again in a given year, they assume a different leadership role.

Because we live in a technologically sophisticated world, parishes need leaders who are comfortable with technology to take a role in intergenerational faith formation. Often the most savvy leaders in this arena are young people. St. Elizabeth of Hungary employed the expertise of a sixteen-year-old who created a DVD on Generations of Faith which the parish shares with newcomers. This helps familiarize them with the intergenerational approach to faith formation without having to repeat the fundamentals at each session.

Many parish leaders who are launching intergenerational faith formation worry about getting enough volunteers. One strategy for recruiting faith formation leaders that benefits both the parish and its parishioners is offering a "Gifts Discernment" process to teenagers, young adults, middle adults, and seniors. Providing them with an opportunity to have their gifts for ministry identified, then matching them with leadership roles that use their gifts, creates a win-win scenario. It gives them something they can use in all areas of their lives. It's also a way to get and keep many volunteers.

Another key strategy for recruiting leaders is tapping into their expertise. St. Elizabeth of Hungary maps out its core themes for its ten monthly intergenerational sessions, then invites people with experience and wisdom in each theme to assume leadership in designing and facilitating that session—but only that session. Barbara Dane shared how much more willing people are to say yes to something for just one month, something that matches their particular passion. For example, the bereavement minister for the parish led the session on the Rite of Funerals; members of the Stewardship Committee led the sessions on stewardship; and the youth of the parish (among the most knowledgeable) led the parish on the topic of justice and service.

The simple wisdom the parish uses is summed up by Barbara Dane in this way: "Don't make it too hard; don't make it too meeting-based. Tap into people's areas of expertise." While there are varied ways of inviting people into leadership (bulletin announcements, an ad on the parish website, display in the gathering space, etc.), nothing is more effective than a personal invitation. This is particularly true for young adults, who often feel disconnected from parish life.

Forming Catechists

Catechist formation is vital to effective intergenerational catechesis. Many catechists who have taught children for years feel intimidated by the idea of teaching adults or teaching mixed generational groups. St. Elizabeth of Hungary Parish uses an apprenticeship model to train catechists. When the parish first began Generations of Faith, the leadership was staff and core-team centered. The staff invited those who had previously been catechists for age-specific groups to become "teaching assistants" for the large-group and break-out sessions the first year. Gradually these assistants took on increasing leadership in planning and implementing the learning sessions. By the fourth year of Generations of Faith, a significant number of leaders came from non-staff members of the parish.

Parishes also take advantage of online training for their catechists. The Center for Ministry Development's Generations of Faith Web site (www. generationsoffaith.org) offers training sessions for catechists on specific themes. The training includes an overview of the learning session, an activity that engages the learner in the topic, a reflection on how the topic connects with the learner's own life, the theological (scriptural and ecclesial) foundations for the topic, personal and professional applications of the topic to the life of the learner, a summary of what has been learned, and suggested resources for further study. One of the advantages of online learning is its flexibility. Catechists choose when and where they do their training.

Another strategy for training catechists is using an already-developed catechetical formation program. *Into the Fields* (Twenty-Third Publications) was created specifically to train catechists for whole community catechesis. It includes a three-part approach: 1) experiencing the Spiritual Exercises of St. Ignatius for spiritual growth; 2) reviewing the Catholic faith through the *Growing Faith Project* booklets; and 3) learning strategies and skills for teaching in various settings from classroom to youth ministry gatherings.

Many Generations of Faith parishes prepare catechists through a "rehearsal" of the intergenerational session. All leaders come together a week or two before the faith festival to walk through the actual learning experience. People who are new to leadership gain confidence in both content and methodology through the practice session.

St. John the Baptist Parish in Mankato uses a variety of resources to form its core team and catechists. The most popular is *United States Catholic Catechism for Adults*. The training of the parish leadership teams, which include older teens, young adults, adults, and seniors, is three-pronged: leaders are given materials to read in advance; they spend time in reflection and prayer; they then do the skills portion of the meeting. They are also given the opportunity to participate in retreats three times a year. Mary Beth Nygaard, Director of Faith Formation, said that they have become a community of faith as a result of their reflection and prayer and learning together.

Creating an Organic Approach

One unique opportunity that presents itself in intergenerational faith formation is using the parish's own charism and circumstances to create learning sessions. Intergenerational learning can and should take on the personality of the parish. The same core teaching will take on different emphasis and different action responses in a rural parish than it will in an urban or suburban parish. Parishes with an ethnic character have a unique opportunity to utilize and celebrate the particular gifts of their culture in intergenerational learning sessions.

LEARNING RURAL-STYLE

Holy Trinity Parish of Webster County, Iowa, consists of eight worship sites, five of them rural and three in the city of Fort Dodge. There are 2,700 families in the parish. Sister Theresa Engel, SSSF, the Director of Intergenerational Faith Formation, described how the parish cluster chose to do a year of intergenerational learning on the theme of "Acting for Justice." In the fall, the Catholic social principle of the option for the poor and vulnerable was the core teaching. To ground the principle in real life, the Social Justice Committee recommended that the parish undertake a project with Catholic Relief Services designed to help developing countries sustain themselves through farming. The Webster County farmers were invited to share their expertise, the use of their machinery, and their time to help farmers in Tanzania. The farmers pledged the profit from a certain number of acres of their land (thirty-six acres the first year, double that in the second year) to go to sweet potato farmers in Tanzania. Parishioners in the city got involved by contributing to the purchase of seeds, gasoline, and fertilizer for the farmers. When the crops were harvested, the parish had raised $11,000 for Tanzania, which was matched by the U.S. government with another $11,000.

At the end of the harvest, the parish held a faith festival of Thanksgiving, which included a prayer service, recognition of the participating farmers, a meal, hayrack rides, rides on combines, and pumpkin painting for the children.

During the winter and spring months, the parish focused on the Catholic social principles of peace, care for God's creation, and solidarity. While the parishioners learned together, they also made donations to help the farmers in the project buy the seeds for their spring planting. On the Rogation Days (April 25 and the three days before the Ascension on which special prayers are said for a bountiful harvest), the farmers' seeds were blessed in anticipation of planting. Later one farmer claimed it was the best crop he'd ever had, and gave credit to the blessing of the seeds by the pastor.

Although the parish moved to a different topic for faith formation in succeeding years, the farming project continues. A local farmer visited Kenya and Ethiopia to meet the farmers there who would be helped by the parish in Webster County! A large poster of a stalk of corn holds a prominent position in the parish, tracking the amount of money the parish has raised on behalf of farmers in Africa.

Learning Across Cultures

There is a significant Southern Sudanese population in Mankato, Minnesota. Consequently, when St. John the Baptist Parish did a Year of Justice in its program, the design team wove the Sudanese people into the session on the Catholic Social Principle of Solidarity. Members of the Sudanese community, who emigrated from the Darfur region, shared their stories, also recounting the difference the faith community of Mankato had made in their lives. Personal relationships between parishioners and the Sudanese community blossomed.

St. John also made use of its local justice experts in fashioning an intergenerational session on Rights and Responsibilities. Speakers included those who worked in Head Start, a local nursing home, and a low-income medical provider. The speakers shared how their faith influenced their work, and thus how faith has influenced the local community.

The Diocese of Victoria, Texas, is predominantly rural. Sister Digna Vela, I.W.B.S., the Director of the Office of Catechetical Ministries, shared two stories of how well intergenerational catechesis meshes with the culture of rural communities. St. Michael and Our Lady of Guadalupe in Cuero, Texas, are the Anglo and Hispanic parishes in a town of about 5,000 people. They used to do their own faith formation. When the parishes moved from two distinct to one shared pastor, the pastor determined that the monthly intergenerational faith formation sessions would rotate back and forth between the two parishes. A yearly theme was chosen, and the two parishes named their shared faith formation the Catholic Community of Cuero. Sister Digna was proud to note that as a result of *Generations of Faith*, the two separate faith communities were united. She also said people may never feel quite ready for launching into something different like intergenerational learning, but they just have to "Do it in faith!"

In East Bernard, Texas, Holy Cross Parish gets about 500 regular participants in its intergenerational faith formation sessions. The total population of the town (not all of whom are Catholic) is 2,000! As Sister Digna notes, rural people are comfortable with coming together and are used to gathering as an intergenerational community. She also noted that the young adults in their twenties in East Bernard are particularly enthusiastic about the intergenerational faith formation.

THE LOCAL IDENTITY

Parishes share stories of using the church building itself to teach. St. John the Baptist Parish in Mankato uses the Perpetual Adoration Chapel to teach the meaning of adoration. Parishes with stained glass windows featuring various saints use the windows to prepare for the Feast of All Saints. Parishes often feature their patron saint in learning sessions. Many parishes that are celebrating an anniversary, building a new worship space, or celebrating the merger of two parish communities use their intergenerational learning sessions as opportunities to prepare their parishioners for these significant moments in parish life.

Motivating Adult Learners

Many parishes have not integrated adult faith formation into their catechetical programs, in spite of the church's vision in the *General Directory for Catechesis*: "Adult catechesis must be given priority" (GDC, #258). The good news from parishes who participated in the *Generations of Faith* project was the finding that inviting adults into intergenerational faith formation is often the springboard for them to demand more catechesis—just for them. They want to go deeper in exploring their faith. Some of these adults are parents who stay with their children for the break-out sessions in order to learn together as a family. But they, too, are asking to be fed spiritually as adults.

St. Mary's Parish in Waverly, Iowa, experienced that awakening hunger in its adults. After two seasons of monthly intergenerational sessions, the adults asked for more. Parents with children wanted more adult-focused learning experiences in addition to the family-based sessions. Unattached adults just hungered for more faith formation. Consequently, an adult Bible study was formed, as was a movie study group in which adult learners analyze the values of contemporary movies through the lens of Catholic morality.

Before Generations of Faith was started at St. Elizabeth of Hungary Parish in Acton, Massachusetts, about twenty adults came to the adult faith-formation programs. They were the same people who went to everything the parish offered. But once GOF began, more and more adults became excited about their faith. Barbara Dane described the increase in adult faith formation as "the hugest part of the GOF program." She noted that adults particularly began to look for more places where they could apply their faith. An adult trip to the Gulf region to provide volunteer aid for victims of Hurricane Katrina was a direct outcome of the intergenerational learning the adults had experienced.

Another benefit to adults at St. Elizabeth came about providentially. The parish took a lectionary-based approach to its intergenerational sessions. When the core team met to design the monthly session, the pastor engaged the team in exegesis around the scripture passage which would be studied by the entire parish. The staff decided to open that meeting to anyone interested. Many of the catechists who would be leading the large or small groups came. But to the joy of the staff, other parishioners, hungry for more knowledge of the scripture, also came. And the members of the staff with a background in theology began to share the leadership for these meetings with Father Walter.

At St. John the Baptist Parish in Mankato, the hunger for further learning led to adults in the parish being offered the opportunity to participate in service days each year. Adults also came together to study gospel themes through contemporary movies, using *Lights, Camera, Faith!* as a resource. St. John now has two annual retreats—one a Mom's Retreat and the other based on Twenty-Third Publication's *Growing Faith Project*.

The more a parish does intergenerational faith formation, the more adults seem to hunger for more faith formation.

HELPING THE ELDERS

A strength of intergenerational catechesis, which is in direct contrast to the practices in our culture today, is the way it honors the wisdom of the elders. The *General Directory for Catechesis* describes the value of the elderly in passing on the faith:

> The Bible presents us with the figure of the old man as the symbol of the person rich in wisdom and fear of God, and as a repository of an intense experience of life, which, in a certain sense, makes him a natural "catechist" in the community. He is a witness to the tradition of faith, a teacher of life, and a worker of charity. Catechesis values this grace. It helps the aged to discover the riches within themselves and to assume the role of catechists among children—for whom they are often valued grandparents—and for young people and adults. Thus a fundamental dialogue between the generations can be promoted both within the family and within the community. (#188)

Intergenerational catechesis provides a forum in which the elders can share their wisdom with younger parishioners. Parishes in the Generations of Faith project report strong attendance by seniors in their faith-formation sessions. St. Elizabeth of Hungary Parish makes a conscious decision to invite its seniors to step up and take a leadership role in Generations of Faith; the response has been very positive. At St. John Brebeuf Parish in Winnipeg, Manitoba, parishioners celebrated the ninetieth birthday of a faithful participant at an intergenerational session. As one family headed home at the end of the evening, the eight-year old boy commented, "Wow! Mercedes is ninety years old and she still comes to catechism class. Wow!"

St. John the Baptist in Mankato has an eighty-year-old on the core team and the catechetical team. Mary Beth Nygaard noted that the challenge for her parish faith formation—keeping seniors involved in meaningful ways—is the challenge of the whole church. She shared that when the annual theme for intergenerational faith formation was a Year of Prayer, the seniors were invited to take the lead on the topic of Catholic devotions. Who better to share the experience of devotions than those who have done them for sixty, seventy, or eighty years?

Keeping Justice at the Core

Parishes doing effective intergenerational learning have discovered that one topic that engages all ages is justice. Perhaps this is because human beings have an innate sense of justice—not just for themselves but also for all of humanity. Justice penetrates so many aspects of our Catholic identity. As the U.S. Bishops wrote in *Communities of Salt and Light:*

> In these challenging days, we believe that the Catholic community needs to be more than ever a source of clear moral vision and effective action. We are called to be the "salt of the earth" and "light of the world" in the words of the scriptures (cf. Mt 5:13–16). This task belongs to every believer and every parish. It cannot be assigned to a few or simply delegated to diocesan or national structures. The pursuit of justice and peace is an essential part of what makes a parish Catholic. (p. 2)

A good practice in intergenerational faith formation is making a justice connection no matter what the theme. It is a natural way to move the community from theory to practice, from talking about their faith to living it in the home and in the world. At St. Elizabeth of Hungary Parish, more and more service and outreach has occurred as a result of intergenerational learning. Since the parish uses the lectionary for its content, the gospels have been the focus for learning. Parishioners hear the challenge of Jesus to serve others; service has been their response. While the youth have had a long track record of serving, now adults are more involved. And Director Barbara Dane sees families giving and serving as families. She says this has "come right out of Generations of Faith."

St. John the Baptist Parish in Mankato is a Stewardship Parish. Because of this, it has been easy for the intergenerational faith formation team to weave the theme of justice into its sessions. Three times over the past several years, stewardship has been the theme of an intergenerational session. Each time a different perspective on stewardship has been shared with the participants, from sharing what stewardship is to holding a stewardship fair to get parishioners involved in giving of their time and talent. Mary Beth Nygaard noted that the year the intergenerational faith formation theme was Creed, it was very easy to weave justice and stewardship into the content. As she said, "It fits into who we are as church."

Holy Cross Parish in Euclid, Ohio, includes service projects as a component of its intergenerational gatherings. The staff sees this as a way to remind people that "church is so much more than people we see on a regular basis." The response from parishioners has been positive. Some of the monthly thematic sessions and the related connection to living out the option for the poor and vulnerable include:

1. Confirmation and the Gifts of the Spirit: simple blankets which are made by tying two pieces of fleece together with knots (created at the intergenerational session) were donated to homebound parishioners, St. Vincent de Paul, A Women's and Children's Shelter, and other agencies

2. Anointing of the Sick: handmade get-well cards were sent to the Hospice of the Western Reserve, Rainbow Babies and Children's Hospital, homebound parishioners and surgical patients

3. Eucharist: loaves of bread were donated to the local hunger center

4. Reconciliation/Putting the Pieces Back Together: jigsaw puzzles were donated to Family Transitional Housing

5. Holy Orders: inspirational cards were sent to local seminarians and priests

6. Marriage: financial donations were made to Katrina victims through Catholic Charities of New Orleans; "Welcome to our Home" door knob hangers were given to newly married couples

7. Discipleship and Service—Walking in the Footsteps of Jesus: new and gently used footwear was donated to the Women's Re-Entry Network, the Men's Mission, and Applewood Centers for Children

8. Catholic Christians in a Diverse World: towels and washcloths were donated to the Interfaith Hospital Network

9. Stewards of the Earth: cash donations were made to the Heifer Project.

Making justice connections to local realities, weaving service into the "at home" phase of the learning process, and increasing parishioners' awareness of the centrality of justice to our Catholic identity are natural outgrowths of effective intergenerational learning experiences.

Non-Traditional Learning Option

Resurrection Parish in Rochester, Minnesota, is a parish that deserves accolades for its creative approach to learning. As the staff processed how they would offer intergenerational learning in their community, they decided that they did not want to offer just another program but a completely different learning opportunity. What they created is "Expanding Horizons."

Expanding Horizons incorporates interactive stations that focus on a core Catholic teaching. These stations are displayed in the parish's great hall for ten days, from Friday to the second Sunday. Parishioners can come any time between 9 a.m. and 9 p.m. The self-guided tour allows participants to learn at their own pace and engage in learning with a spouse, child, friend, neighbor, or individually. There are three levels of activities: adults (grade 10 and older), youth (grades 5-9), and children (grades 1-4). The stations for children are designed for parent/child learning.

All forms of media are utilized in conveying information. The creative and artistic ability of the design team is limited only by space and time. On entering the great hall, participants sign in and pick up a guide pamphlet that explains the layout and gives basic directions. Display boards prompt the reader with intriguing questions, present lists of interesting facts, or provide numbered tasks to complete the designated activity. Collages and posters are often stunningly arranged in a museum style. Short video clips and CD players herald music, recite poetry, or tell stories. Shadow boxes allow for viewing of precious objects. Framed religious pictures placed on easels tell a story. Journals are available for jotting down questions for the pastor, or for a participant to comment on what was learned, or to share additional information with future participants. Worksheets, word searches, flash cards, and puzzles test parishioners' knowledge. Instructional booklets are constructed for those who want detailed information. A Resource table showcases current books and periodicals that address the topic, and additional handouts are made available. There are even unique areas for meditation on a theological question with the opportunity to express one's insights.

Expanding Horizons was developed at Resurrection in response to needs expressed in their intergenerational session evaluations.

Parishioners were saying, "I don't like sharing my faith with others because I feel I don't know enough." "The intergenerational session (Parish Night) did not fit with our household schedule; we need more flexibility." "I'm uncomfortable in a large group setting." And, "The intergenerational session alone does not provide enough time to adequately teach and experience the topic."

In the first year, the parish positioned Expanding Horizons a week or two before their intergenerational learning sessions (Parish Night), to prepare the parish for the intergenerational learning session. It gave parishioners an opportunity to think ahead and ruminate on the ideas and information presented. Resurrection hoped this exposure would not only stimulate thought and prayer, but also facilitate the parishioners' comfort level in sharing their faith experiences and insights at the other intergenerational offerings. This supposition proved accurate when on Parish Night participants would verbally refer to their Expanding Horizons experience during discussion periods.

Attendance at Expanding Horizons is not as large as at the structured intergenerational learning events, and space constraints do not permit keeping the displays up for longer than a ten-day period in the great hall. To accommodate those who cannot attend during the ten days, they have consolidated some of the elements of the displays into a single smaller display. It is placed in a quiet but noticeable corner of the main gathering space.

Due to the time required for team catechesis, planning, design, and sometimes construction, Resurrection found that the design and implementation team (thus far seven to nine people) is only capable of creating three Expanding Horizons a year without compromising variety and quality.

The first year the theme was prayer. The three Expanding Horizons were:

1. Lord's Prayer: Origins and Liturgical Development; Seven Petitions; Trinity. Used mainly poster displays and instructional materials on tables with CD for listening to the Lord's Prayer sung by a local singer.

2. The Rosary: History; Four Mysteries; Mary's Role; Catholic Tradition. Created a museum environment. Artwork and scripture passages announcing four sets of Mysteries were

positioned around perimeter. Chairs and kneelers were available for viewing and reflection. Large rosary display with descriptions of rosaries with personalized stories of their significance in the lives of parishioners.

3.   Catholic Devotions: Saintly Influences, Prayer Styles, Catholic Culture. Converted the space into a home layout where they explored "The Sacred in our Ordinary Life" by traveling through each room and interacting with questions proposed. Each room and hallway focused on a specific Catholic Devotion.

In the second year Resurrection's theme was sacraments. The three Expanding Horizons focused on:

1.   Sacraments of Initiation

2.   Sacraments of Healing

3.   Sacraments of Vocation

Conclusion

Creating a well-trained, diverse leadership team that includes gifted people from the ages of 16 to 76, and preparing catechists for sharing faith in an intergenerational context are two best practices that set parishes up for effective catechesis. Taking a general theme of Catholic identity and making it real by applying the core teaching to life on the local level is another. A concrete sign of success in intergenerational learning occurs when the adults—many of whom have not had catechetical experiences since they were children—express a hunger for more. Challenging parishioners to move their learning from head and heart to the hands and feet through service not only makes the learning stick—it transforms the whole community. And thinking outside the box to help parishioners learn their faith in a diversity of ways is a must in today's hectic world.

Whatever the practice, parishes who have embraced intergenerational faith formation have found it to be worth the effort. And for some of them, intergenerational learning, in the words of Mary Beth Nygaard, "has become part of our culture."

End Notes

Center for Ministry Development. www.generationsoffaith.org subscription Web site.

Huebsch, Bill, editor. *Into the Fields*. New London, CT: Twenty-Third Publications, 2006.

Congregation for the Clergy. *General Directory for Catechesis*. Washington, DC: USCCB, 1997.

United States Conference of Catholic Bishops. *Communities of Salt and Light*. Washington, DC: USCCB, 1993.

An Event-Centered Curriculum

Church Year Feasts and Seasons

> The history of salvation, recounting the "marvels of God" (*mirabilia Dei*), what he has done, continues to do and will do in the future for us, is organized in reference to Jesus Christ, the "center of salvation history." (GDC, #115) (See also GDC #85, 97–98, 101–102, 105, 108.)

> Who has encountered Christ desires to know him as much as possible, as well as to know the plan of the Father which he revealed. Knowledge of the faith (*fides quae*) is required by adherence to the faith (*fides qua*). Even in the human order the love which one person has for another causes that person to wish to know the other all the more. Catechesis, must, therefore, lead to the "gradual grasping of the whole truth about the divine plan," by introducing the disciples of Jesus to a knowledge of Tradition and of scripture, which is "the sublime science of Christ." (GDC, #85)

FOUNDATIONAL EVENTS	POTENTIAL THEMES
Advent season	Salvation history
Christmas season	Incarnation
Lenten season	Discipleship and conversion Praying, fasting, almsgiving
Triduum	Paschal mystery, salvation, redemption
Easter season	Resurrection
Ascension-Pentecost	Mission
Sundays of Ordinary Time	Reign of God, teachings and deeds of Jesus

Sacraments

The sacraments, which, like regenerating forces, spring from the paschal mystery of Jesus Christ, are also a whole. They form "an organic whole in which each particular sacrament has its own vital place." In this whole, the Holy Eucharist occupies a unique place to which all of the other sacraments are ordained. The Eucharist is presented as the "sacrament of sacraments." (GDC, #115) (See also GDC #85, 108.)

Christ is always present in his church, especially in "liturgical celebrations." Communion with Jesus Christ leads to the celebration of the salvific presence in the sacraments, especially in the Eucharist. The church ardently desires that all the Christian faithful be brought to that full, conscious, and active participation which is required by the very nature of the liturgy and the dignity of the baptismal priesthood. For this reason, catechesis, along with promoting a knowledge of the meaning of liturgy and sacraments, must also educate the disciples of Jesus Christ "for prayer, for thanksgiving, for repentance, for praying with confidence, for community spirit, for understanding correctly the meaning of the creeds…," as all of this is necessary for a true liturgical life. (GDC, #85)

FOUNDATIONAL EVENTS	POTENTIAL THEMES
Baptism	Initiation, conversion, mission: priest, prophet, king
Confirmation	Conformity to Christ, witness, discipleship
Eucharist	Meal, sacrifice, real presence of Christ
Reconciliation	Repentance, sin, conscience
Anointing of the Sick	Healing, suffering, hope, resurrection
Marriage	Covenant love, fidelity, vocation
Orders	Vocation, service, mission

Justice and Service

Jesus, in announcing the Kingdom, proclaims the justice of God: he proclaims God's judgment and our responsibility.…The call to conversion and belief in the Gospel of the Kingdom—a Kingdom of justice, love, and peace, and in whose light we shall be judged—is fundamental for catechesis. (GDC, #102) (See also GDC #86, 102–104, 108.)

Catechesis is also open to the missionary dimension. This seeks to equip the disciples of Jesus to be present as Christians in society through their professional, cultural and social lives.… The evangelical attitudes which Jesus taught his disciples when he sent them on mission are precisely those which catechesis must nourish: to seek out the lost sheep, proclaim and heal at the same time, to be poor, without money or knapsack; to know how to accept rejection and persecution; to place one's trust in the Father and in the support of the Holy Spirit; to expect no other reward than the joy of working for the Kingdom. (GDC #86)

JUSTICE THEMES	POTENTIAL EVENTS
Life and dignity of the human person	Respect Life Sunday, saint feast days, service and justice/advocacy projects (local and national), and Sunday lectionary readings
Call to family, community, and participation	Holy Family Sunday, election day, service and justice/advocacy projects (local and national)
Dignity of work and rights of workers	Labor Day, feast of St. Joseph the Worker
Rights and responsibilities of the human person	Thanksgiving, World Hunger Day, Migrant and Refugee Week, service and justice/advocacy projects (local and national), and Sunday lectionary readings
Option for the poor and vulnerable	Thanksgiving, Lent, Poverty Awareness Month, Feast of St. Vincent de Paul and other saints, service and justice/advocacy projects (local and national), and Sunday lectionary readings
Solidarity	Lent, Pentecost, Mission Sunday, sponsoring a development project (e.g., Catholic Relief Services)
Care for God's creation	Earth Day, Feast of St. Francis, action projects (local, national, international)
Peace	World Day of Peace (January 1), Martin Luther King Jr. Holiday, saint feast days, national and international peace projects

Prayer and Spirituality

The Our Father gathers up the essence of the Gospel. It synthesizes and hierarchically structures the immense riches of prayer contained in Sacred Scripture and in all of the church's life. (GDC, #115) (See also GDC #85, 108.)

Communion with Jesus Christ leads the disciples to assume the attitude of prayer and contemplation which the Master himself had. To learn to pray with Jesus is to pray with the same sentiments with which he turned to the Father: adoration, praise, thanksgiving, filial confidence, supplication, and awe for his glory. All of these sentiments are reflected in the *Our Father*, the prayer which Jesus taught his disciples and which is the model of all Christian prayer. The *"handing on of the Our Father"* is a summary of the entire Gospel and is therefore a true act of catechesis. When catechesis is permeated by a climate of prayer, the assimilation of the entire Christian life reaches its summit…. (GDC, #85)

FOUNDATIONAL THEMES	POTENTIAL EVENTS
Forms of prayer (blessing and adoration, petition, intercession, thanksgiving, praise)	*Sunday Mass, Lent—practice of prayer, Holy Thursday, Good Friday, Stations of the Cross, World Day of Prayer, praying with the saints (feast days)*
Expressions of prayer (vocal, meditation, and contemplation	
Lectio Divina; *Liturgy of the Hours*	*Praying in Advent and Christmas, Lent, Holy Week, and Easter seasons*
The Lord's Prayer	*Sunday Mass, 17th Sunday in Ordinary Time (C)*

FOUNDATIONAL THEMES	POTENTIAL EVENTS
The Rosary	Marian feasts, praying the rosary through year: joyful (Christmas), sorrowful (Holy Week), glorious (Easter), luminous (Ordinary Time)
Catholic prayers and devotions	Sign of the cross, Stations of the Cross, Eucharistic adoration, devotion to the saints

Creed

The Apostles' Creed demonstrates how the church has always desired to present the Christian mystery in a vital synthesis. This Creed is a synthesis of and a key to reading all of the church's doctrine, which is hierarchically ordered around it. (GDC, #115) (See also GDC #85, 99–100, 108.)

Who has encountered Christ desires to know him as much as possible, as well as to know the plan of the Father which he revealed. Knowledge of the faith (*fides quae*) is required by adherence to the faith (*fides qua*). Even in the human order the love which one person has for another causes that person to wish to know the other all the more. Catechesis, must, therefore, lead to the "gradual grasping of the whole truth about the divine plan," by introducing the disciples of Jesus to a knowledge of Tradition and of scripture, which is "the sublime science of Christ." By deepening knowledge of the faith, catechesis nourishes not only the life of faith but equips it to explain itself to the world. The meaning of the creed, which is a compendium of scripture and of the faith of the church, is the realization of this task. (GDC, #85)

FOUNDATIONAL THEMES	POTENTIAL EVENTS
We believe in one God...	*Trinity Sunday, Easter Vigil, Easter Season, Rite of Baptism*
We believe in one Lord, Jesus Christ...birth, mysteries of Christ's life, death, and resurrection	*Christmas, Baptism of the Lord, Transfiguration, Triduum, Sunday lectionary readings*
We believe in the Holy Spirit...	*Easter season, Pentecost, Rite of Confirmation*
We believe in one holy catholic and apostolic church...	*Easter season, Pentecost, feast of Saints Peter and Paul*
We acknowledge one baptism for the forgiveness of sins...	*Rite of Baptism, Easter Vigil*
We look for the resurrection of the dead, and the life of the world to come...	*All Saints, All Souls*

Morality

The double commandment of love of God and neighbor is—in the moral message—a hierarchy of values which Jesus himself established. "On these two commandments depend all the Law and the Prophets" (Mt 22:40). The love of God and neighbor, which sums up the Decalogue, is lived in the spirit of the Beatitudes and constitutes the *magna carta* of the Christian life proclaimed by Jesus in the Sermon on the Mount. (GDC, #115) (See also GDC #85, 97, 104, 108.)

Conversion to Jesus Christ implies walking in his footsteps. Catechesis must, therefore, transmit to the disciples the attitudes of the Master himself. The disciples thus undertake a journey of interior transformation, in which, by participating in the paschal mystery of the Lord, "they pass from the old

man to the new man who has been made perfect in Christ."
The Sermon on the Mount, in which Jesus takes up the
Decalogue, and impresses upon it the spirit of the beatitudes,
is an indispensable point of reference for the moral formation
which is most necessary today....The moral testimony, which is
prepared for by catechesis, must always demonstrate the social
consequences of the demands of the Gospel. (GDC, #85)

FOUNDATIONAL THEMES	POTENTIAL EVENTS
Love of God, neighbor and self (Commandments 1-4)	Sunday lectionary readings, e.g., Great Commandment (30th Sunday of OT, cycle A), Sermon on the Mount (4th–9th Sundays of OT, cycle A), Sermon on the Plain (6th–8th Sundays of OT, cycle C), parable of the Good Samaritan
Respect for human dignity (Commandment 5)	Christ the King—cycle A, Sunday lectionary readings, saint feast days (see justice events and themes)
Justice (Commandments 7 and 10)	Sunday lectionary readings, Sermon on the Plain (6th -8th Sundays of OT, cycle C), parable of the Rich Man and Lazarus (see justice events and themes)
Faithfulness (Commandments 6 and 9)	Sacrament of Marriage, World Marriage Day, Wedding Feast at Cana, Sunday lectionary readings
Honesty and integrity (Commandments 8 and 10)	Sunday lectionary readings, saint feast days
Care, compassion, forgiveness	Lectionary readings of Jesus' actions, gospel stories, such as the prodigal son and the woman caught in adultery, saint feast days

Summary of Key Research Findings

Background Information

Generations of Faith is a project of the Center for Ministry Development that is designed to help parishes implement faith formation with the intergenerational community. The project included parish team training, consultation, and resources for intergenerational faith formation. Leadership for the Generations of Faith project was provided by the Family and Intergenerational Ministry Team of the Center for Ministry Development:

- John Roberto, Project Coordinator
- Leif Kehrwald
- Mariette Martineau
- Joan Weber

Generations of Faith was funded through a grant of the Lilly Foundation.

A qualitative research method was used to identify the perspectives of parish leaders regarding the GOF project and the factors that contributed to change. The outcomes of this research complement the quantitative research process, which focused more explicitly on the evaluation of the GOF project.

The qualitative research was conducted by the Center for Ministry Development staff with consultation from Richard E. Morehouse of Viterbo University.

In their book, *Beginning Qualitative Research*, the consultants for this project, Pam Maykut and Richard Morehouse describe this research method as follows: Qualitative research is a research model that "*examines people's words and actions in narrative or descriptive ways as experienced by the participants*" (p. 2). To accomplish the aims of the evaluation, the research was focused on the experience of parishes who have implemented intergenerational faith formation using the resources of the Generations of Faith project.

The qualitative research was conducted in the following nine dioceses with a total of 83 parishes:

Albany, 11 parishes
Boston, 12 parishes
Buffalo, 8 parishes
Cleveland, 10 parishes
Dubuque, 11 parishes
Green Bay 11 parishes
Joliet, 8 parishes
Phoenix, 11 parishes
Winona, 11 parishes

Every parish involved in the study had been implementing intergenerational faith formation using the resources of the Generations of Faith project for at least one year. In each of the nine dioceses, there were two focus group interviews conducted along with one or two in-depth parish interviews.

The following lists of questions were used as guides for the group interviews.

- When you chose to participate in the GOF project, what were your hopes for faith formation in your community?
- Describe faith formation in your community now:
    What has changed?
    What has remained consistent?
    What do you think still needs to change?
    If needed: Take me to your parish when your community is sharing

faith. When intergenerational faith formation is happening, what do you see? What do you notice? What do you hear?

- What were the factors or conditions in your community that helped you create dynamic faith formation?
- What conditions were challenging in your community?
- What are the practices that you implemented that have supported your innovations? In other words, what have you started doing or stopped doing that helped you be successful?
- How did the GOF project help your community in developing your faith formation?

    What do you think were the strengths of the GOF project? What were the weaknesses?

- How has your involvement with intergenerational faith formation affected you personally or professionally? In other words how has this project affected you as a leader or as a person? When you think of your community, what gives you hope?

Each interview was transcribed from the tapes to a written transcript. These transcripts formed the basis of the research compilation. The full transcripts were coded to identify the group interview site and group. These transcripts were then duplicated for the data analysis. To prepare for the data analysis, each member of the research team read the transcripts of the interviews that she/he conducted.

To analyze the data, the research team "unitized" the data (isolating parts of the transcripts from which a particular theme or topic emerged.) The research team read all of the transcripts and then began the process of sorting the data and arriving at the outcomes or findings. Throughout the process of data analysis the team worked to stay close to the data so that they truly honored and respected the voices of the people interviewed.

The research team worked with the findings and the quotations to determine the "Key Findings." This process included examining the prominence of factors within the transcripts as well as the importance and salience of the findings as they related to our focus of inquiry. The teams worked to identify the most important findings and then to identify other findings that were related to or supportive of these key findings.

Additional findings that were not related to the "Key Findings" were left to stand on their own.

The Key Findings from the qualitative research were then put into a quantitative survey to allow a broader base of GOF leaders to express their level of agreement or disagreement with the findings. Practitioners from over 430 parishes responded to the survey.

The material found on the following pages summarizes all the findings from the qualitative research interviews integrated with the levels of agreement/disagreement as tabulated in the quantitative research. The material is categorized as follows:

- Readiness
- Intergenerational Learning
- Leadership
- Impact
- Effectiveness

Readiness
FINDINGS FROM QUALITATIVE RESEARCH

1. Parish leaders hoped that lifelong faith formation would provide a way for families to learn and share faith together—at the parish and at home.

2. Parish leaders hoped that lifelong faith formation would increase participation in the events and ministries of the parish.

3. Parishes realized that the "classroom model" of faith formation did not work well in their parishes.

4. Parishes identified a number of factors already present in parishes that contributed to their readiness to move toward lifelong faith formation:
   a) experience with family programming,
   b) an empowering mindset on the part of leaders,
   c) good liturgy,
   d) hunger for learning,
   e) confidence in parish leadership by the parish community, and
   f) willingness on the part of parish leadership to try new things.

RESULTS FROM QUANTITATIVE RESEARCH

Survey Question 16: A number of factors already present in parish life, have surfaced as important to the readiness of the parish to implement GOF and lifelong catechesis. Please rate how important each of the following readiness factors were in your parish's implementation of GOF. (1 = not important; 5 = very important)

4.34 Parish staff empowers people

4.27 Confidence in parish leader

4.15 Good liturgy

4.13 Willingness to try new approaches

4.00 Hunger for learning in the parish

3.16 Prior experience with family programming

Participation

(Connection to and Participation in the Life of the Parish)

FINDINGS FROM QUALITATIVE RESEARCH

1. Successful implementation of lifelong faith formation involves concerted efforts to integrate lifelong faith formation with all existing parish programs and ministries.

2. The faith formation addressed within GOF learning programs connects with many aspects of parish life and promotes faith sharing at home.

3. GOF prepares people for greater participation in the liturgical and sacramental life of the parish.

4. Participation in intergenerational learning led to greater involvement in parish life, including the liturgical and sacramental life of the parish, justice and service projects, and parish ministries.

Results From Quantitative Research

PARTICIPATION RATES:
HOUSEHOLD PARTICIPATION BY PARISH SIZE

% OF HOUSEHOLDS	UNDER 750	750-1500	1501-2500
10% or less	23.5%	36.8%	42.2%
11-20%	30.6%	34.6%	31.3%
21-30%	22.4%	19.9%	16.9%
31-40%	12.9%	7.4%	7.2%
41-50%	7.1%	.7%	0%
Over 50%	3.5%	.7%	2.4%

PARTICIPATION RATES:
NUMBERS OF PARTICIPANTS

TOTAL NUMBER	PERCENT AND NUMBER OF PARISHES	
Under 250	62.4%	(271)
251-500	21.7%	(94)
501-750	9.4%	(41)
750-1000	3.9%	(17)
1001-1250	.5%	(2)
1251-1500	.5%	(2)
1501-1750	.7%	(3)
1751-2000	.5%	(2)
2001-2250	.2%	(1)
2250-3000	0	
3000 and over	.2%	(1)

PARTICIPATION RATES:
NUMBERS OF PARTICIPANTS BY PARISH SIZE

TOTAL NUMBER	UNDER 750	750-1500	1501-2500
Under 250	87.6%	50.7%	44.6%
251-500	10%	31.6%	28.9%
501-750	1.8%	3.7%	15.7%
751-1000	.6%	0	8.4%
1001-1250	0	0	0
1251-1500	0	0	1.2%
1501-1750	0	0	0%
1751-2000	0	.7%	1.2%

Intergenerational Learning
FINDINGS FROM QUALITATIVE RESEARCH

1. There is involvement of all ages and generations—parents and children, teens, young adults, adults, older adults, and whole families—in faith formation through intergenerational learning. It is still a challenge to involve certain groups in the parish, such as Catholic school families, young adults, and single adults.

2. Intergenerational relationships are created as people of all ages learn from one another and grow in faith together.

3. Intergenerational learning strengthened the parish community— through relationship building and participation in church life. People take time to talk and share with one another.

4. Participation in intergenerational learning led to greater involvement in parish life, including the liturgical and sacramental life of the parish, justice and service projects, and parish ministries.

5. Intergenerational learning addresses a hunger that adults have to learn more about their faith and fill in the gaps in their formation. More adults are participating in faith formation.

6. Families enjoy opportunities to pray, learn, and be together. Families are growing in the ways that they share faith.

7. Intergenerational learning creates an environment in which participants feel safe to learn, ask questions, and grow in faith on a deeper level.

8. Participants are engaged in a variety of learning activities that are experiential, multi-sensory, and interactive. Faith sharing and personal experience are an important element of learning.

9. Adequate parish meeting space plays a key role in conducting successful intergenerational learning programs.

10. Intergenerational learning is exciting—the enthusiasm, joy, and energy are attractive and contagious.

11. Some GOF parishes are succeeding in their efforts to have parents learn alongside their children, while parents in other parishes express a preference for "adult only" learning.

Leadership
FINDINGS FROM QUALITATIVE RESEARCH

1. Successful implementation of lifelong faith formation depends on the participation and investment of the whole parish staff and ministry leaders, not just those involved in faith formation.

2. The active support and involvement of the pastor, as evidenced by encouragement, an empowering style, long-term commitment, and advocacy, is important for the effective implementation of lifelong faith formation.

3. It is essential to have a coordinator who fully understands the vision and can work with others to implement it.

4. Effective teams have a shared vision for implementation and practice teamwork and collaboration.

5. Lifelong faith formation requires a large number of committed volunteer leaders, and parishes are discovering talented and resourceful people in their community.

6. A large number of committed volunteer leaders are engaged in a variety of roles in lifelong faith formation: planning, teaching,

organizing, and supporting. Many parishes are discovering talented and resourceful people to help with GOF.

7. Volunteer leaders are empowered and trusted to take responsibility for key aspects of the implementation of lifelong faith formation. It cannot be done by staff alone.

8. Through their participation as leaders in lifelong faith formation, leaders feel closer to God, grow in their knowledge of the Catholic faith, and have more confidence in sharing it with others.

9. GOF leaders benefit from networking, sharing, and problem solving with other parishes.

10. GOF provides experiences for team members that are creative, hopeful, energizing, growth-filled, and committed.

Impact

(Intergenerational, Household, and Leadership)

RESULTS FROM QUANTITATIVE RESEARCH

Survey Question 17: The following statements describe the impact of GOF on a parish community and its leaders. Please indicate your parish's degree of agreement with each statement. (Rating: 1 = strongly disagree; 5 = strongly agree)

4.26 Intergenerational learning engages participants in a variety of learning activities that are experiential, multi-sensory, interactive, and involve faith sharing.

4.21 Through their involvement in GOF, volunteer leaders grow in their knowledge of the Catholic faith and their sharing it with others.

4.17 GOF leadership teams share common vision for GOF and its implementation in the parish.

4.06 Families benefit from intergenerational learning through opportunities to pray, learn, and be together. Families are growing in ways that they share faith.

4.0 Intergenerational learning strengthens the parish

community through relationship building and participation in parish life; people take time to talk and share with each other.

3.98   Intergenerational learning provides an environment in which participants feel safe to learn, ask questions, and grow in faith on a deeper level.

3.97   Intergenerational learning addresses a hunger that adults have to learn more about their faith.

3.92   Families are growing in faith and developing ways to share their faith through intergenerational learning.

3.92   Through their involvement in GOF, volunteer leaders feel closer to God.

3.76   Our parish is reaching new audiences, such as adults and whole families, through intergenerational learning

3.73   Intergenerational relationships are created through intergenerational learning, as people of all ages learn from one another and grow in faith together.

3.69   Participation in GOF learning programs leads to greater involvement of participants in parish life, including Sunday Mass, sacraments, service projects, and in the ministries of the parish.

3.57   There has been an increase in the number of adults participating in faith formation because of intergenerational learning.

3.45   Families are growing in faith and sharing faith at home by using the home kit or other materials along with their learning from the intergenerational session.

Effectiveness
(Intergenerational, Household, and Leadership)

RESULTS FROM QUANTITATIVE RESEARCH
Survey Question 18: Please rate the quality or effectiveness of GOF in your parish using the following statements. (Rating: 1 = poor; 5 = excellent)

3.95   How would adults rate the overall quality and experience of the intergenerational learning programs?

3.87   How would you rate the quality of collaboration and teamwork among the GOF leadership teams?

3.84   How would families with children rate the overall quality and experience of the intergenerational learning programs.

3.75   How would the parish staff and key ministry leaders rate the overall effectiveness of GOF?

3.48   How would the adults rate the quality and usefulness of the home kit or home materials?

3.45   How would families with children rate the quality and usefulness of the home kit or home materials?

3.37   How would you rate your parish's efforts in equipping (training, resources) leaders for their roles in GOF and trusting them to take responsibility for GOF?

3.12   In addition to intergenerational learning programs, how would you rate your parish's efforts to prepare the whole community for a church event?

3.10   How would you rate your parish's efforts in developing a variety of leaders necessary for the effective implementation of GOF?

3.06   How would middle school and high school youth rate the overall quality and experience of intergenerational learning programs?

MARIETTE MARTINEAU serves as a project coordinator on the Family and Intergenerational Ministry Team at the Center for Ministry Development. She coordinates Generations of Faith Online, Fashion Me a People, and is a faculty member of the Institute for Lifelong Faith Formation. Mariette co-authored the *Celebrating the Sacraments* and *Responding in Prayer* intergenerational sessions and magazines for the *People of Faith: Generations Learning Together* series from Harcourt Religion Publishers. Mariette and her husband, Dean, live in Kenora, Ontario, Canada with their three children.

JOAN WEBER is a member of the Family and Intergenerational Ministry Team at the Center for Ministry Development. She coordinates the Institute for Lifelong Faith Formation and the Young Adult Ministry Services at the Center. She holds a Master's degree in Pastoral Ministry with a Theology Emphasis from Creighton University, a Certificate in Advanced Studies in Ministry Development, and a Certificate in Faith and Justice. Joan co-authored the *Celebrating the Sacraments* and *Responding in Prayer* intergenerational sessions and magazines for the *People of Faith: Generations Learning Together* series from Harcourt Religion Publishers.

LEIF KEHRWALD has worked in family ministry and faith formation on the parish, diocesan, and national levels for thirty years. Currently, he is a project coordinator on the Family and Intergenerational Ministry Team at the Center for Ministry Development. Leif has published several books and numerous articles on family life, family ministry, marriage, lifelong faith formation, and youth ministry. His latest book is *Families and Faith: A Vision and Practice for Parish Leaders* (Twenty-Third Publications, 2006). Leif has taught courses on family ministry, family spirituality, and parish faith formation at Loyola University Chicago, University of Dayton, and Mount Angel Seminary in Oregon. Leif and his wife, Rene, have two young adult sons and live in Portland, Oregon.